WINCHESTER
From Prehistory to the Present

WINCHESTER
From Prehistory to the Present

TOM BEAUMONT JAMES

TEMPUS

To Peter, recalling many happy hours in Winchester

Front cover: Winchester Cathedral Choir. *Image by permission of John Crook*

Back cover: Reconstruction drawing of Roman Winchester buildings. Coloured buildings are reconstructed at The Brooks (foreground) and Woolworth's site, High Street (centre). The Forum buildings (top) ran west and south of the site where The Pentice stands today, covering the whole width of the Roman High Street. *By permission of the artist, Dr Philip Marter*

First published 1997 by Batsford and English Heritage
This extended and revised edition 2007

Tempus Publishing Limited
The Mill, Brimscombe Port,
Stroud, Gloucestershire, GL5 2QG
www.tempus-publishing.com

British Library Cataloguing in Publication Data.
A catalogue record for this book is available from the British Library.

ISBN 978 0 7524 3742 2

Typesetting and origination by Tempus Publishing Limited
Printed in Great Britain

CONTENTS

ACKNOWLEDGEMENTS

A study of 4000 years of Winchester's development inevitably requires a range of specialist expertise beyond the ken of an individual. Those with knowledge of wider and narrower aspects of Winchester's past have been unfailing in their unselfishness in providing materials and answering questions and I offer them, once again, my heartfelt thanks. In particular Martin Biddle (Winchester Research Unit) and staff of the Winchester Archaeology Office have read drafts, and have supplied illustrations. I am particularly indebted to Graham Scobie, who has thought long and hard about Winchester's development, and Ken Qualmann with his special knowledge of the Roman city. Barry Cunliffe and John Collis kindly commented on specific chapters in 1996. John Crook has been a great support in many different ways through the preparation of both editions.

At the University of Winchester I wish to thank managers for continuing to support local and regional studies in many different ways including the funding of some illustration permissions by the Research and Knowledge transfer Committee for this edition. Colleagues in archaeology and history have read critically and have generously answered questions from their own expert knowledge, especially Professor Tony King and Professor Barbara Yorke. My research students and undergraduates have lit new areas from their work, and I thank them. Since the first edition was published postgraduates in my Winchester Project have completed a significant group of doctoral studies on post-medieval Winchester: Mark Allen (the coming of the railway, 1999); Justine Cooper (the High Street 1750-2000, 2001); Peter Crossley (corporation leases in the nineteenth century, 2003); Michael May (city probate inventories $c.1650$-$c.1710$, 1998); Craig Pinhorne-Smy (GIS study of central Winchester in the twentieth century, 2001) and work is nearing completion by Karen Parker on probate inventories ($c.1500$-75), and by Chris Grover on suburbs ($c.1850$-1914) and others besides. These studies make a great new contribution to our knowledge of Winchester, and their contributions to knowledge are signposted in the text below, although limited space has precluded any more than passing references in all cases. Mark Allen has kindly read the modern chapters, contributed to them from his own depth of knowledge of the city and the period, has saved me from errors, and has joined the directors of the Winchester project to push studies of the city forward.

For the first edition Ann Bailey sought illustrations. Barbara Bryant, Martin Henig, Edward Roberts, with whom I subsequently published an article on the late medieval city, and Elizabeth Proudman among many others all offered expert insights. Illustrations are individually acknowledged, but I should particularly like to thank John Crook both for illustrations and his great patience in dealing with photographic materials, also Judith Dobie, Alejandra Gutiérrez, Victoria Ling and Philip Marter. Peter Kemmis Betty, formerly at Batsford and now at Tempus, encouraged me to update and rework the book for new and previous readers alike. Tom Vivian has guided matters forward at Brimscombe Mill.

All my family remain models of support to me. My son Edward revealed many mysteries of computing and helped with the index; my sister Elisabeth Barton kindly re-typed the original text for me. My wife, Muffie, remains patient as ever. I thank them unreservedly.

In the knowledge that it is not possible to reconcile all areas of debate, I take responsibility for the text published here.

Tom Beaumont James
March 2007

PREFACE

This is a revised and updated version of the book originally published in 1997 by Batsford and English Heritage. I have taken the opportunity to include occasional references to recent archaeological and historical work on Winchester especially that which has appeared out of the mainstream: in newsletters and postgraduate theses for example. The text is refined with new insights and perspectives which have emerged over the last decade and takes account of further reflection over the last decade. We know more than we did ten years ago.

The study of Winchester is unique because progress has been made towards integration of so many sources at all periods, but especially in the complex Saxon and medieval periods in which archaeology, architecture, documentary and scientific analysis have all been pursued. The work of the Winchester Excavations Committee, and its successor the Winchester Research Unit, has been of key significance over half a century, not only in archaeological recording, but also in laying the foundations for study of topography and documents. More recently the work of the Winchester Museums Service, including both archaeologists and museum staff have added greatly to our detailed knowledge of the city's past.

This study introduces the major trends and results as presently known. From the author's point of view, documents, buildings, prints, drawings and photographs are as much artefacts as are pottery, environmental evidence and other products of earth archaeology. So far as is possible in a text of this length, themes have been traced through built environment, population and social structure, economy and religion. These are set in the context of archaeology and history.

1

WINCHESTER:
HERITAGE REVIEWED

WHY WINCHESTER?

Winchester has a place in every history of England, most commonly as the 'ancient capital' associated with Saxon kings. Its status and royal heritage made it a focus in civil wars: the siege of 1141 caused much destruction as did the struggle of king and parliament in the 1640s when its castle, that symbol of royal rule for half a millennium, was smashed by artillery. Thus its fortunes have been mixed. In the late 1980s, however, it was regarded as the richest city in Britain. Today it comes top of a survey of the best places to live in Britain.

The city has been studied not only as a Roman settlement, as was usual in the post-war period, but since 1961 as an urban phenomenon through time (*1*). Archaeological excavation and historical surveys have illuminated the development to the city from the Saxon period onwards. This is particularly evident in a seminal series of monumental books unique in British archaeology: Winchester Studies. Combining archaeology, architecture, history and science, these studies comprise an unrivalled, integrated approach which has set Winchester apart from other cities.

It is only in the twentieth century that archaeology, as a professional endeavour, has added depth and new dimensions to antiquarian and historical studies. The monuments stay the same, but examination of their context through digging and post-excavation analysis has produced some extraordinary results: archaeology's contribution is discussed in the chapters that follow.

THE FIRST RECORDS

There is little documented reference to Roman Winchester. The first is Ptolemy, writing in Alexandria *c*.AD 150, drawing on older information. Saxon accounts, especially the *Anglo-Saxon Chronicle*, are helpful in providing a chronology – if not always an accurate

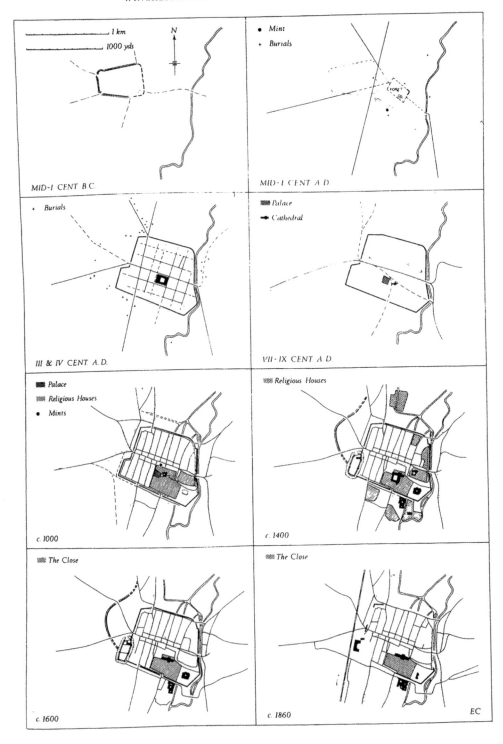

1 Eight phases of Winchester's development showing interpretations based on evidence collected to c.1988. Modifications to that understanding are noted on pp.45 and 52. *Copyright Winchester Research Unit*

one – for events such as the conversion to Christianity, the founding of the minsters and Viking attacks. Also, names of individual historical personages, such as Bishop Swithun (died 861x3; see also pp.58-60) and King Alfred (died 899) are mentioned (see Chronology pp.177ff). Manuscript and pictorial evidence which can be specifically associated with Winchester, amounting to products of a first 'Winchester School', survives from the time of Alfred onwards. Administrative sources such as the Burghal Hidage (p.52) provide insights into the defences and reorganisation of the city in the ninth and tenth centuries.

Although Domesday Book (1086) was kept in Winchester, no survey of the city of that date now exists. However, surveys of c.1110 and 1148 exist, and these include significant retrospective material from which much about the city either side of the Conquest of 1066 can be deduced. For example, in the matter of names we learn that there was one 'William' in a sea of Old English names recorded from pre-1066 in the survey of 1110, by which date there were 14 (6.1 per cent of those named) and by 1207 39 Williams, (10.2 per cent). The surveys show how Continental names triumphed over Old English ones, as, for example, the English Cypping named his sons Hugo, Roger and Radulf while fathers such as Brand and Westman (Old Norse names) called their sons Girard and Herbert (von Feilitzen 1991, 185-9). This data and very much more besides has been published in the Winchester Studies volumes. The twelfth century witnessed the flowering of a second 'Winchester School' which produced the exquisite Winchester Bible, not only the greatest treasure of the cathedral library today, but also an important element of medieval world heritage. Conceived on a huge scale, like so many grand medieval projects including cathedrals themselves, it was never finished. However, the illuminations are sumptuous, the work of many artists, some from as far away as Spain.

National administrative records, notably those of the exchequer, begin c.1150. Winchester appears incidentally in these and in the records of the writing office, the chancery. These official records, housed at The National Archive, Kew, contain much detailed material about royal administrative preoccupations, such as visits to (and repair of) the castle and taxation accounts. The latter provide a basis for population figures, derived for example from the poll taxes of 1377-81. The fine series of city charters begins in the mid-twelfth century, concerned with the ancient privileges and town government (the gild merchant: see Glossary). A secondary series of charters from the fifteenth and sixteenth centuries deals with various forms of economic aid.

Charters form the basis of the city liberties and some are preserved among the city archives at the Hampshire Record Office (HRO), Sussex Street in Winchester (see 85). From the thirteenth century the city authorities began to generate records of its government, legal and financial affairs, including its land holding. By 1417 Winchester city owned a large body of property, which increased substantially after the Reformation (see *colour plates 11* and *12*). Other institutions, including monasteries, the Hospital of St John, Winchester College and St Cross (a cartulary was rediscovered there in 1994), also held lands and their tenants were recorded.

Post-Conquest chronicles and annals report events in the city. They build on (and often build up) the Saxon and Norman history of the city, frequently making it hard, and sometimes impossible, to determine what happened when.

TRAVELLERS, GENTLEMEN AND ANTIQUARIANS

Administrative records were written and kept for technical reasons, for example to apportion responsibility for taxation or as records of rent or repairs. Medieval chronicle writers rarely travelled far from their religious houses. They presented evidence that they had heard, or read in earlier accounts, which they developed for their own purposes. Thus the lives of King Arthur, Swithun and Alfred, scantily recorded by their contemporaries, developed later as legends.

In the fifteenth century and thereafter, the increasingly diverse administrative records continue to be very important, and include new sources such as the probate inventories which detail the contents of individual properties room by room (see for example Keene 1985, ii; May 1998). They are supplemented by eyewitness accounts by visitors and antiquarians which provide 'snapshots' of the city as it was at different periods, and furnish individual responses to the city previously only available through sources devised for other purposes. John Leland visited in 1540-1, just after the Dissolution of the monasteries. He found the city walled, with six gates, and refers to a dozen or so religious houses. Three of the suburbs were 'litle'; the eastern one – The Soke – was bigger, with two parish churches, St Peter Chesil and St John, both of which stand today.

The seventeenth century produced the first map of Winchester, by John Speed (2). But if there were gains, there were significant losses as well, especially in the cathedral archives where soldiers twice devastated the ancient records, the Chapter clerk recording 'writings and Charters burnt, divers thrown into the river' others, 'divers larg parchmentes' being made into kites 'to flye in the Aire' (HCC 1997). John Trussel, a local and historian of Winchester, witnessed the Civil War. A royalist, twice mayor and a comparative newcomer, Trussel (died *c*.1648) was interested in the city's history and wrote *The Touchstone of Tradition*, a useful, if inaccurate, account of the early history of Winchester (Atkinson 1963). The Restoration of 1660 revived interest in the city's past. William Schellinks, a Dutch topographical artist, visited in 1662. He admired recent additions to the cathedral, such as Inigo Jones's screen, now demolished, with its statues of James I and Charles I, which survive. His drawing of Winchester, displayed as a print at the Hampshire Record Office, dominated by the ruined castle keep, shows the city as he described it: 'within … wide walls, which are now, like the castle, badly damaged. [The city] is large, but only thinly populated.' Henry Hyde, second earl of Clarendon, uncle of queens Mary and Anne, was a courtier who completed in 1683 *Some Account of the Tombs and Monuments in the Cathedral Church of Winchester*, to which was added a catalogue of cathedral charters compiled by deputy record keeper at the Tower of London, Hyde's work and the catalogue were published in 1715.

Celia Fiennes, writing in the mid-1690s, clearly indicates the condition of the city, which had had its hopes of renewed royal status raised by Charles II, but dashed by his death in 1685. She tells us much about the built environment: the streets, 'pretty good, large and long, the buildings but low and old.' She admired the new houses in The Close and a model of the proposed royal palace, but was disappointed to see the palace itself unfinished. Fiennes, on the whole, deprecated historic or outmoded elements of

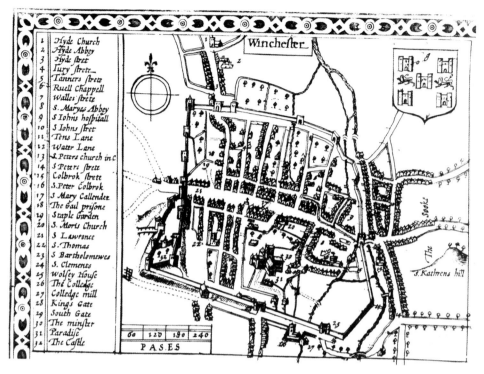

2 Speed's plan of *c.*1611, enlarged from an inset on his map of Hampshire. North of the High Street, the Brooks area, comparatively bare of houses, contrasts with the flourishing eastern suburb. *Photograph John Crook; copyright: Hampshire Record Office, 139M89, vol.1, p.3*

the city. The cathedral and especially its monuments, Wolvesey (which her description suggests she did not visit), the ruined castle, the old-fashioned paths and the potted plants of the Deanery garden were all criticised. But not everything old disappointed her: Winchester College chapel, cloister and library, the Renaissance replacement tomb chests of the Saxon kings and the choir stalls in the cathedral she found appealing (Fiennes 1695/1982).

EIGHTEENTH- AND EARLY NINETEENTH-CENTURY VISITORS AND ANTIQUARIANS

Daniel Defoe (*c.*1725) was struck by the antiquity of Winchester, 'not only the great church … but even the whole city has at a distance the face of venerable and looks ancient afar off'. He found the lack of decoration on the exterior of the cathedral disappointing and the structure 'plain and coarse', but he praised modern buildings: Winchester College 'School' by Wren (p.140) and the new buildings at Wolvesey Palace, both built in the late seventeenth century. He was appalled at the ruination of the medieval bishop's palace at Wolvesey. He liked local society, both clergy and gentry (Defoe, 1731/1964).

A group of Cambridge gentlemen visiting in 1735 were, by contrast, impressed with the cathedral, dubbing it 'magnificent', and listed the memorials to bishops with enthusiasm. They commented on the mixture of good and bad housing 'which contribute nothing to Beauty', though they were struck by the cleansing brooks which flowed openly though the streets. The following year saw the Buck brothers' panorama of Winchester (3) which records the city as the Cambridge gentlemen must have seen it.

The first measured map of Winchester was published in 1750 by William Godson (see 68 and 69). The border shows certain important buildings and monuments, some of which Godson had surveyed for individuals and the corporation in an album produced at the same time (see *colour plate 13*). The first Winchester guidebook appeared in 1773, five years after its Southampton counterpart, and two years ahead of Portsmouth (Oldfield 1993, 3). Not long afterwards, Winchester, always traditional in its ways and with a Catholic community, welcomed John Milner as its priest in 1788. Ten years later Milner began to publish *The History, Civil and Ecclesiastical, and Survey of the Antiquities of Winchester* (1798–1801), a major contribution to our knowledge of the ancient capital's past. Milner served in Winchester until 1803 in which period he saw the building of the 'Milner Chapel', one of the first Gothic revival buildings in England, as a proper setting for Catholic worship (1792). In addition, he encouraged the physical excavation of Winchester's medieval and Catholic past, for example in the castle area in 1797, although he was horrified at the maltreatment of the remains of Hyde Abbey, the resting place of King Alfred (*colour plate 5*), which at that time was being used as the site of a new county gaol, whose prisoners are credited with the excavation, desecration and loss of the great king's bone (Patten 2001; Gerrard 2003, 29; www.winchester.gov.uk for the Hyde excavations).

Milner's contemporary in the city, the scholarly schoolmaster the Reverend Dr Richards at Hyde, appears to have concentrated his interests on the then unfashionable Elizabethan and early Stuart period, collecting statuary and other objects and installing an extraordinary ceiling of *c.*1620 in his school at Hyde. He and Milner would have had much to discuss and share in their antiquarian interests spanning catholic and early protestant pasts in the city (Gapper, Parker and Roberts 2002, 59–80). At this same period John Lingard was born at Winchester in 1771. Lingard became a priest and a Catholic historian and although struggling hard to be 'impartial' in his efforts to present his *History of England*, which began to appear in 1819, to a protestant readership, none the less believed Luther to be diabolical!

William Cobbett visited *c.*1830 and like his predecessors went to the cathedral, 'that ancient and most magnificent pile', in particular to show his son, Richard, the tomb of William of Wykeham (died 1404). Richard asked 'Why, papa, no one can build such places now, can they?' 'No, my dear,' replied Cobbett, 'that building was made when there were no poor rates; when every labouring man was clothed in good woollen cloth; when all had plenty of meat and bread and beer.' Such a conversation was characteristic of the enthusiasm for the Middle Ages, a feature of the incipient Gothic Revival, in which medieval architecture and life were favourably compared with that of the nineteenth century. Augustus Pugin, a generation later, praised Milner as a herald of the revival of interest the Gothic past (4 and see Gapper *et al.* 2002). After viewing the

3 The Buck brothers' panorama of 1736 shows Winchester College and the ruins of Wolvesey (left). Grand houses bracket the cathedral: (left to right) a new, grand house of 1730 at 26/27 St Swithun Street; houses in The Close and Wolvesey; Charles II's palace with Southgate Street below it and Pescod's Abbey House beside The Broadway. The lower High Street is flooded, symbolic that for all the grand houses, Winchester was largely in decay in the early eighteenth century. North of the High Street, Penton's House dominates the residences which sprang up in St Peter Street and in the north-west area of the city. The eastern suburb flourishes. The Soke, Sir Thomas Fleming's early seventeenth-century house appears old-fashioned with its timber-frame (left) beside St Peter Chesil church. *John Crook*

cathedral the Cobbetts went outside the city to the north, where they were horrified to see in Hyde Meadow a county Bridewell (prison) occupying the site of Hyde Abbey, where Alfred 'that maker of the English name' had one been buried. But Cobbett was no friend of the clergy when he spoke to freeholders at Winchester, before he fled to America in 1817. Cobbett attacked the clergy as Christ's gamekeepers, living in palaces with parks stocked with deer 'and gardens coming up to Mahomet's idea of Elysium'. The churchmen present, not surprisingly, barracked him (Biddell 1999, 19).

THE VICTORIANS

Such public interest as that displayed by Cobbett was mirrored by academic interest in the monuments of the past. This enjoyed a platform in 1845 with the meetings in the city of the British Archaeological Association in August and its rival, the grander Archaeological Institute, in September. 'The room was crowded with fashionable company, among whom were many ladies,' trumpeted the *Illustrated London News*. A single national organisation held a preliminary meeting at Canterbury in 1844 but had split in acrimony over the perennial question for archaeologists – publication, hence the two meetings at Winchester. The spirit of competition which characterised the

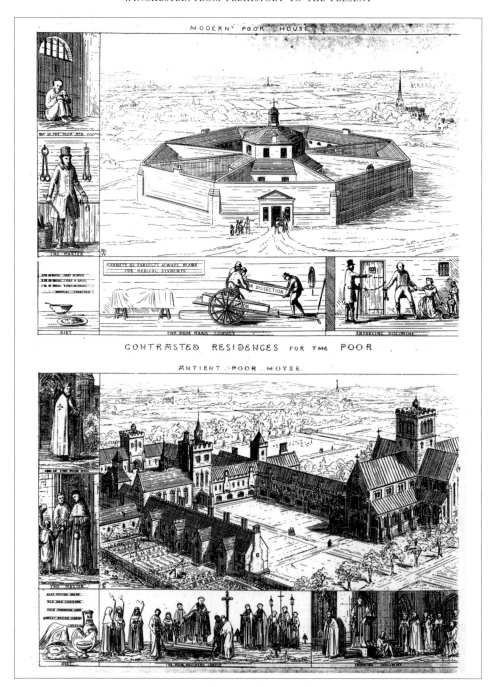

4 Contrasted residences for the poor. Like Cobbett, Pugin unfavourably contrasted nineteenth-century experience with medieval in his vision of a pure Catholic past. As in the same work, he did not label his representation of a Catholic medieval city as Salisbury, so he does not refer to the Hospital of St Cross, Winchester seen here as his model of medieval poor-relief. He may have been unaware that St Cross was not only the focus of a financial scandal around 1800, but was rebuilt in the fifteenth century not for local poor, but for retainers of the aristocratic Cardinal Beaufort. *Pugin, A.W., Contrasts, second edition, 1846*

Winchester meetings did, at least, stimulate interest in the city's history and antiquities. The speakers at the Archaeological Institute included Professor Willis, on the cathedral (5), Edward Hawkins on the ancient mint and exchange at Winchester, Sir Thomas Phillipps, J.G. Nichols, T.H. Turner and others (Archaeological Institute, 1846; see Bibliography for contributors).

The rapid publication of the proceedings, and the clear tide of public interest, was accompanied in 1846 by a proposal to found a museum. A meeting in October that year at the Corn Exchange resolved to found a museum for natural objects and also for materials illustrative of 'the customs, manners, and fashions of past years'. The museum started life in Hyde School House as a county venture, but became the City Museum in 1851, in which year there were 2000 visitors. The curator from 1847-71 was Henry Moody. It moved to the vacant house of the governor of the county gaol in Jewry Street, and thence to the new guildhall in 1874. A second museum, which still operates, was opened in the West Gate in 1898.

The Ordnance Survey produced a large-scale map of the city in 1872, on which many of these buildings can be identified. The gentry who had encouraged the museum were again active in the establishment of the Hampshire Field Club and the Archaeological Society in 1885, which still regularly publishes primarily archaeological, architectural and historical material.

THE COMING OF THE PROFESSIONALS

The twentieth century saw the tradition of observing the city and noting chance finds translated into a policy of organised, intrusive excavation supported by a growth in museum provision. An early stage in this change of emphasis was the establishment in 1903 of a new City Museum in The Square, created by Alderman Jacob's Museums Committee. This was one of the very first purpose-built museums in the country.

Twentieth-century figures did not merely read about or observe ancient sites in the city, they dug them up on an unprecedented scale. Some of this work has been 'research', such as Martin Biddle's excavations (6) of the 1960s, described recently as 'most novel and influential in ethos and technique' (Gerrard 2003, 98). These excavations took place near the cathedral, at Wolvesey, at the castle and elsewhere. They were original in scale, with an average of 170 people on site during a 14-week season, as well as in technique, from the open-area excavation seen in figure 8 to the integration of documentary work and science (Keene 1985; Gerrard 2003, 119-20). Biddle's 'research' excavations were seen as 'elevated' over 'rescue' excavations in the city, such as the City Archaeologist's work at Woolworth's or the International Stores in the High Street, or the Brooks excavations on 1987-8 (see 7; Biddle 1968; Gerrard 2003, 99).

Between the wars archaeology was overseen by Sydney Ward-Evans (died 1943), the city's 'honorary archaeologist'. Ward-Evans was an amateur who had been encouraged by Edith Wilde, then honorary curator of the City Museum and herself an authority on the city's historic weights and measures. Observation by Ward-Evans of demolition

5a The British Archaeological Institute met in the finely decorated St John's Rooms, formerly a medieval hospital, on The Broadway in September 1845. The Lely portrait of Charles II, now in the Guildhall, is above the dais; the speaker seen here with the wand was probably Professor Willis, famous for his detailed work on English cathedrals, as seen in figure *50*. *Author's collection*

5b The same room in 1983. *Copyright RCHME*

sites and holes in the fabric of the city was invaluable for future archaeologists. Working unpaid and on his own he began to map out the city's archaeological past, depending for sustenance on donations of food from the *Hampshire Chronicle*, for whom he wrote. On the Iron Age site at St Catharine's Hill, J.N.L. Myres, a former Winchester College schoolboy and subsequent lecturer at Christ Church, Oxford, undertook excavations with C.F.C. Hawkes, which were published by Hawkes in 1976.

Meanwhile at the museum, honorary curators were succeeded in 1947 by a professional. The first bolder of that post was Frank Cottrill, who served for over 25 years until his retirement in 1973. He organised the collections and instigated an increasingly systematic archaeological study of the city and district involving small-scale excavations which began in 1949 (WMS 2001b). Cottrill, and his wife Eleanor, who was the county archivist, brought about a transformation in the study of Winchester's past. Eleanor had worked previously in Leicester, and brought especial vigour to the interdisciplinary work of archives, archaeology (her appointment was championed by O.G.S. Crawford), and museums (HCC 1997). Frank Cottrill was well connected in archaeology. He had worked with Mortimer Wheeler before the war and had taken over Gerald Dunning's position examining the archaeology revealed by building development in London, and like Dunning was a drawer of pots. He knew Kathleen Kenyon from Leicester, where he worked before coming to Winchester.

Sprung from the tradition of inter-war archaeologists, Cottrill saw that a new generation had to be encouraged. Three of these young men have since become professors of archaeology. In the 1950s John Collis was still a schoolboy when Cottrill encouraged him to excavate; Barry Cunliffe was another young and talented Hampshire archaeologist who came to excavate in Winchester before 1960. Martin Biddle was a Cambridge undergraduate, excavating a Roman villa in Twyford, when he met the curator and was invited by the city authorities to excavate the site of the Wessex Hotel in 1961 (6). Even in 1961 nothing certain was known of the origins of Winchester (WMS 2001b).

Biddle, encouraged by Roger Quirk's remarkable prediction of the sites of the Saxon Minsters, then formed the Winchester Excavation Committee and excavated for a further 10 seasons until 1971. In Cottrill's time work at Winchester came to command major and national attention.

Since 1972, the post of city archaeologist has been filled by Kenneth Qualmann, who has continued to excavate, largely in a rescue capacity, as rapid development has engulfed the city. Since 1990, rescue archaeology has stopped as government-funded excavation has given way to commercial backing under the recommended guideline known as PPG 16. Archaeology is now planning-led.

Digging, driven by excavation seasons, limited funds and developers' necessity to begin building, is over comparatively quickly. The products of the excavations (plans, sections, photographs etc. as well as the finds themselves) require detailed expert analysis, and often demand as least as much funding as the original excavation to prepare and publish the results. The records and finds are all to be found in the care of the Winchester City Museum Service, where Elizabeth Lewis, an authority on timber-framed buildings, was curator from 1973-96.

6 Martin Biddle on the Wessex Hotel (cathedral car-park) site in 1961 preparing an archaeological plan of a burial from the New Minster cemetery. *Copyright Winchester Research Unit*

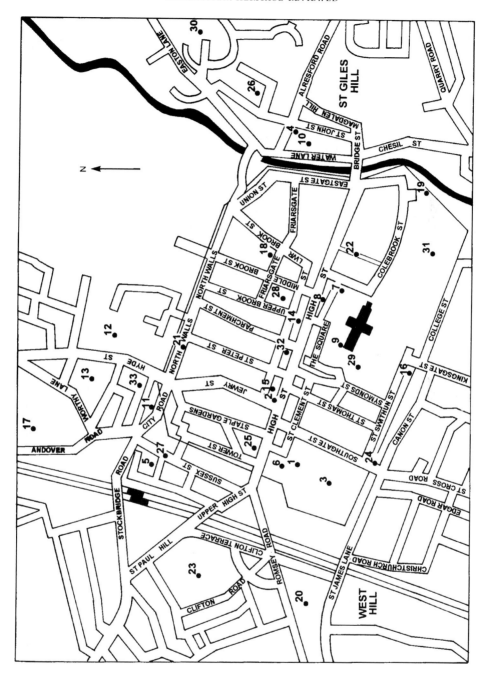

7 Map of Winchester identifying archaeological sites and streets (drawn by Philip Marter). Key: 1. Assize courts. 2. Barclay's Bank (George Hotel). 3. Barracks. 4. Blue Boar. 5. Carfax. 6. Castle Yard. 7. Cathedral car-park. 8. St Maurice church. 8. Cathedral Green. 10. Chester Road. 11. City Road. 12. Hyde Abbey. 13. Hyde Street. 14. International Stores. 15. Kingdon's Workshop and back of Royal Oak. 16. Kingsgate Street. 17. Lankhills. 18. Lower Brook Street. 19. Magdalen Almshouses. 20. Mews Lane. 21. North Walls. 22. Nunnaminster (St Mary's Abbey) and Abbey Passage. 23. Oram's Arbour. 24. Southgate Street. 25. Staple Gardens. 26. St Martin's Close. 27. Sussex Street. 28. The Brooks. 29. The Close. 30. Winnall. 31. Wolvesey Palace. 32. Woolworth's. 33. Victoria Road.

8 Work in progress in 1964: Lower Brook Street, looking south-west. This area revealed domestic accommodation of post-Norman Conquest date (House XIII shown here). Biddle pioneered open excavation: the baulks are still in place at this stage, with tags identifying the stratigraphy. *Copyright: Winchester Research Unit, 3021A*

MAJOR EXCAVATIONS

The locations of major excavations in the twentieth century are shown in *7*. This select summary is designed to help the reader through the maze of local terminology, by relating sites mentioned in the text to periods and excavators. See Bibliography under the excavators' names for reports and interim reports, also under Collis and Scobie.

Prehistoric sites
St Catharine's Hill (Hawkes and Myres before 1930)
Oram's Arbour (Erdberi) and Staple Gardens (Biddle 1964-7; Qualmann 1990s)
Carfax (Qualmann *c.*1985)
Twyford Down (Qualmann and Wessex 1993-4)

Roman sites
St George Street (pre-1955; Cunliffe 1955-7)
Cathedral Green – the forum (Biddle 1961-70)

Lankhills (Biddle/Clarke 1967-72)
Wolvesey (Biddle 1963-71, 1974)
International Stores, High Street (Qualmann 1987-8)

Saxon sites
Winnall (Meaney and Hawkes 1960s)
The minster sites on the Cathedral Green and at the Wessex Hotel (Biddle 1961-70)
St George Street (Cunliffe 1950s)
Nunnaminster (Qualmann *c.*1980)
Staple Gardens (Qualmann 1990s)

Medieval sites (c.1050-1550)
Housing and churches at the Brooks (Biddle 1962-71 (*8*); Qualmann 1987-8)
St George Street (Cunliffe 1960)
Wolvesey Palace (Biddle 1963-71, 1974)
the Castle (Biddle 1962-3, 1967-71; Qualmann 1980s, 1990s)

THE CONTRIBUTION OF ARCHAEOLOGY

Archaeology has deepened our understanding of the city's past, for the prehistoric and Roman periods we depend on archaeology for evidence. There is nothing to see on the surface of the Iron Age site at Oram's Arbour (Erdberi), and yet excavation and non-intrusive methods, such as resistivity survey, have provided a mass of information (p.27ff). At St Catharine's Hill earthworks are upstanding (see *11*), but only by excavation could they be elucidated. The increasingly sophisticated techniques of science and typology have furnished us with date-ranges for evidence from the earth. Structures such as the Saxon minsters have been rediscovered after centuries underground.

Knowledge of the city's past has been sharpened by excavations which have uncovered some 5 per cent of the city's archaeology, according to present knowledge of both the historic area and the depth of deposits. Winchester excavations may not be equal to the area which has been exposed for example in York, but work in Winchester began comparatively early.

The range of materials discovered at Winchester and the depth of the analysis which sets archaeology in a proper perspective of history, architecture and other disciplines, are major achievements of British scholarship. In the pages that follow, the extent to which archaeology with associated disciplines has broadened perceptions of the city's past is highlighted. In this study there is a place for royal Winchester, for its major monuments and exotic finds. Equally there is a place for more overly archaeological topics: suburbs, houses and the built environment, industry, commerce, diet, funerary practice and burial.

2

PREHISTORY AND VENTA BELGARUM TO C.AD 450

LANDSCAPE AND LOCATION

This chapter looks at the prehistoric landscape of the Itchen Valley and the engineered landscape occupied by Venta Belgarum. It was the Romans who made Winchester unequivocally urban. Archaeology has provided proofs of that urban identity: a concentration of population, a complex economic and social structure, organised religion and an influence over the area beyond its walls.

Winchester is at a narrow point on the flood plain of the river Itchen, with the chalk hills rising both to the east (St Giles) and the west (West Hill) (*9, 10*). Prehistoric population occupied the higher ground, perhaps attracted to the area by a fordable place in the river, yet deterred from the valley-bottom sites by marshy land of the kind still seen when walking south of the city through the Meads towards St Cross. The valley bottom was composed of a series of islands amid meandering streams that constituted the Itchen, which may have been navigable in light crafts from the sea to this point.

PRE–IRON AGE

So far as is known, the vicinity of Winchester was not a focus of population in the early Neolithic period. There is a marked increase in activity in the form of flint and stone tools and Beaker pottery from the later Neolithic and earlier Bronze Age both within the walled area and on the surrounding hills, for example: a Beaker vessel found in 1892 at Mews Lane west of the city. Significant increase in settlement evidence to the east of Winnall, to the south at Twyford Down, and on the West Hill, is suggestive of foci of activity including agriculture, domestic occupation and burials, beginning around 2000 BC and continuing into the Later Bronze Age (see Chronology, p.177).

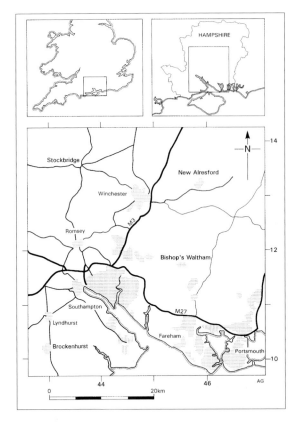

9 Location maps of Winchester. *Drawn by Alejandra Gutiérrez*

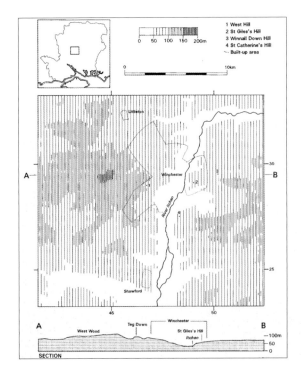

10 Contour plan of Winchester showing east–west cut. *Drawn by Alejandra Gutiérrez*

THE IRON AGE

Evidence for the Early Iron Age (700-300 BC), from the area of the later walled city and its immediate vicinity is predominantly agricultural: field systems, plough soils and a grain-drying hearth. People settled sparsely on the chalk downs, for example to the west of the present city, in the Middle Iron Age, *c.*300-100 BC. The slopes of the Itchen valley continued to be used for agriculture.

Two major foci of Iron Age settlement developed, at St Catharine's Hill to the south of the present city and at Oram's Arbour, which was referred to in medieval documents as 'Erdberi' (Earthbury), to the west. St Catharine's Hill is a hillfort, Erdberi an enclosure at the junction of a north–south route west of the Itchen, with an east–west hill trackway (*colour plate 1* and *10*). Within Earthbury, remains of cultivation lynchets are found; even today, within the north-west corner of the walled city, properties west of Staple Gardens in the Cross Street area are built on the remains of lynchets: the pedestrian negotiates short flights of (modern) steps which carry down from one lynchet to the next (Graham Scobie pers. comm.).

ST CATHARINE'S HILL

St Catharine's Hill was and is encircled by Iron Age earthworks (*11*). Iron Age pottery and artefacts excavated there were published in 1930 (p.24). It was demonstrated through dated pottery types that the entrance to the hillfort was destroyed by fire and the site

11 St Catharine's Hill from the air in 1969. The Iron Age earthworks are clearly visible, together with their landscape of ancient fields. Compare this with *colour plates 1* and *12*. *Copyright Winchester Research Unit*

abandoned at the end of the Middle Iron Age, perhaps about 100 BC. The hillfort dominated the eastern side of the valley of the Itchen. By the time that the pottery sequence ends on the hill, a corresponding pottery series had been established on the west side of the valley at Erdberi. It has been suggested that, as elsewhere, the higher eastern community at St Catharine's Hill, was defensive, the lower western community, at least in the Early Iron Age (700-300 BC), unenclosed. Was St Catharine's Hill ever residential, or was it a refuge in time of crisis? It was probably a centre of economic exchange comparable with the hillfort at Danebury, the best-known analogous site in Hampshire. However, as excavations concentrated on the defences, the nature of occupation inside the earthworks of St Catharine's Hill remains unclear.

ERDBERI (ORAM'S ARBOUR)

There were settlers across the river from St Catharine's Hill in and around Oram's Arbour from the Early Iron Age to the beginning of the Middle Iron Age (600-300 BC). Excavations at Carfax, north-west of the city, for example, revealed rectangular (2 x 3m/6 x 10ft), structures built with upright wooden poles and associated with gullies, possibly field boundaries, suggestive of a mixed economy.

Excavation has revealed that this area, north-west of the city, was enclosed between *c*.300 BC and 100 BC. Ditches and their upcast banks, no longer obvious to view, have been sectioned and dated by pottery. The Middle Iron Age settlement (300-100 BC) at Oram's Arbour is significant in both the length (1.7km/1.06 miles) and the scale of the rampart and ditch (*c*.7.25m/24ft wide and perhaps 4.25/14ft deep) of the defending earthworks. This enclosure was 20ha (50 acres) in area, which made it one of the prime defensive earthworks in southern Britain, equivalent in area, if not in defences, to sites such as Maiden Castle in Dorset.

The Arbour enclosure may have brought together disparate farmsteaders who had settled in that area, possibly to create a more easily accessible refuge than that across the river at St Catharine's Hill. However, the creation of such a substantial earthwork is strongly suggestive of some driving force behind it, for example of a tribal leader. Such an interpretation accords not only with ancient writers, but also with recent arguments about Iron Age social structure put forward by Barry Cunliffe, who knows Winchester archaeology well.

Towards the eastern end of the Oram's Arbour enclosure, a comparatively dense occupation pattern of the Middle to Late Iron Age (300 BC-AD 43) was discerned on the Staple Gardens site, where roundhouses and other structures, in the sequence of occupation, were excavated. In the Late Iron Age (after 100 BC) there was some industrial activity which was later buried beneath the western part of the Roman settlement (*12*), but a higher concentration of activity has been found to the south, outside the enclosure.

Iron Age coinage, such as an Atrebatic piece (early first century AD: see Glossary) found in the north-west quarter of the city, may have circulated in Winchester as money, although there is a possibility that such objects were expensive gifts perhaps distributed

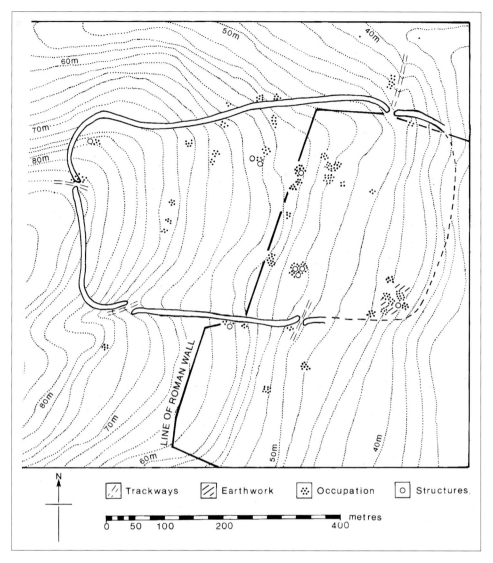

12 Oram's Arbour (Erdberi) Iron Age enclosure. Excavations have revealed additional entrances at the north-east and north-west with associated trackways (cf. 1) and broader occupation patterns. *After Qualmann 1993; redrawn by Judith Dobie; copyright English Heritage*

by tribal leaders. Extended economic links and complex trading activity are indicated by Ptolemaic and Gaulish coins (the latter paralleled at Hayling Island temple to the south-east), remains of sea-fish, querns from Lodsworth (West Sussex) and regional pottery types.

Links with the Continent in the Late Iron Age led to the arrival in the area of the Belgae from northern France or Belgium, who were to give Venta Belgarum (now believed to mean 'market place of the Belgae') its name. Whether they came as economic migrants, invaders, or as refugees from Caesar's invasions of the first century BC is still

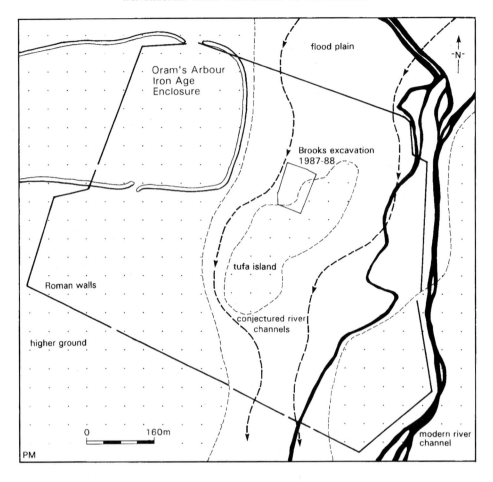

13 The river Itchen originally flowed further westwards than today (cf. 1), around one or more islands. The southern boundary of the Iron Age enclosure at Oram's Arbour may have abutted the western bank of the river, in the area east of the present St Peter Street. *After Qualmann 1993; redrawn by Philip Marter*

debated – especially as Belgic pottery, which would give substance to the place-name theory, has not been found at Winchester. That the Romans chose Venta Belgarum as their name for Winchester suggests that they believed the Belgae had occupied this area. Perhaps, more significantly, if this was the market place of the Belgae, then the site of that market was probably Oram's Arbour.

The extent of the Oram's Arbour enclosure, and its functions, are still being explored, in particular its eastern boundary now buried beneath the area of the later walled city. East of St Peter Street (*13* and see *7*) the natural geology below archaeological layers has never been seen and a steep slope there may prove to be the eastern limit of the Iron Age enclosure.

Oram's Arbour is difficult to categorise precisely: it is not a hillfort, neither does it meet all the criteria to be an *oppidum* or major enclosure. Although dominating a river crossing, it was perhaps enclosed substantially earlier than the first century BC, the usual date assigned to the foundation of British *oppida*.

THE END OF THE IRON AGE

While some evidence survives of industrial occupation on part of the Arbour site in the period immediately before the Roman invasion of AD 43, the enclosure experienced a reduction in permanent settlement in the Late Iron Age. No evidence has yet been found that it was a centre for trade or religion at that period. Its impact on the planning of the early Roman settlement resulted from the existence of the Arbour's large earthworks.

Work at Berwick Fields to the north-west of the city has identified Late Iron Age roundhouses, trackways and grain storage pits, with continuity into the Roman period. Pits and field systems were also found at Twyford Down. Maybe with the abandonment of St Catharine's Hill and the scaling down of the Arbour, there was a slackening of centralised control which led on the one hand to the scattering of population, and on the other made society more vulnerable to Roman invasion. The recent discovery near Winchester of a nationally-important collection of Iron Age gold including torcs (necklaces) of woven gold wire and dating from *c.*80-30 BC, the period of the invasion by Julius Caesar, have illuminated a very rich element in the local culture, even an individual leader and his family. But whether this extraordinary treasure was buried as a votive offering in a long-vanished grove, or was hidden in woodland as fears of invasion or uncertainty resulting from rumoured deals with the Roman Empire spread, will never be known (WMSN 43, 2002).

THE ROMANS ARRIVE

Following the invasion of AD 43, Winchester became one of the first Roman settlements: the evidence suggests a date of *c.*AD 50 for Roman occupation on the west bank of the Itchen and on a tufa (see Glossary) island in midstream. Characteristic straight roads were built by the Romans north toward Cirencester; in time six Roman roads radiated from Venta Belgarum. The layout of these roads particularly to the north of the city (see *1*) may hold clues for the transition from Iron Age to Roman settlement. Perhaps within decades of the invasion, and at the latest by AD 200, the Romans diverted the Itchen and bridged it to the east of their settlement, ensuring the future of Winchester as a centre of communication by road north–south and east–west across the river at the then lowest bridging-point. The Roman bridge and its attendant gate at Winchester, to the east of the city, were sited further south than the present city bridge, probably at a previous ford crossing (see *13*).

Excavations have shown a sequence of Roman settlements at Winchester, but conclusive evidence of an early Roman fort has not been found. Early Roman Winchester interlocked with, and in part overlaid, its Iron Age predecessor in the north-western area of the city. The settlements used the same north entrance (see *12* and *13*), but whether the Romans made any use of the Iron Age defences is unknown.

DEFENCES

The first Roman ditch and rampart defences ran along the northern, western and southern sides of the city; the location of the eastern defences, if there were any at this early date, is uncertain. The western bank and ditch included a 60 x 245m (200 x 800ft) salient where the defences jutted out south of the western entrance to the city at the highest point (*13*). The reason why there was such a considerable deviation in the otherwise largely regular defences is a mystery. The salient is Roman in date, for excavations at the Castle Yard in the 1960s established this beyond doubt. Also within the salient, remains of a building with a tessellated floor were observed in 1683 by Sir Christopher Wren. The salient respected a structure yet to be identified, but it is uncertain whether this was a house, evidenced by tesserae, for a Roman administrator before the *civitas* (see below) was established after *c.*AD 70, or a military area (although little military evidence has been found), or possibly even a theatre.

The extent of the first Roman defences is also uncertain, but a number of phases have been revealed by excavations, notably at South Gate, which suggest a foundation date of AD 75 (*14*). One of the anomalies of Winchester's street plan within the walls is that the north and south gates lay so far west of the city defences (see *13*). This suggests that the early Roman defences were focused further west than their later Roman and medieval successors. It seems likely that the early earthwork defences were part of a broad symmetrical settlement towards the west of the area, eventually walled in. In about AD 60, timber buildings on at least one site between the High Street and St George Street were consumed by fire and early deposits sealed by a burnt layer. Excavation suggests that the eastern banks of the Iron Age enclosure may have been levelled, or that the burnt structures marked the eastern limit of the early Roman settlement.

The defences of *c.*AD 75 were amplified and extended by a second series of earthwork defences, *c.*AD 180-200, which included protection along the river on the east and which completed the circuit. A stone wall was cut into them in third century and medieval walls engulfed Roman ones in numerous campaigns of rebuilding. The line of the Roman walls is found in property boundaries today, to the east at The Weirs, where a scrap of Roman walling is displayed. Fourth-century bastions were discovered at South Gate (1971). Garden walls between St Swithun Street and Canon Street follow the line of the southern Roman walls, and continue on the north side of College Street; also, north of the city at North Walls similar boundaries follow the line of the walls (see *7*).

CIVITAS STATUS

The break-up by the Romans of the extensive kingdom of Togidubnus, a client king of theirs, may have been the catalyst for the development of Venta Belgarum as the urban focus of a *civitas*, or Roman administrative regional centre, and as a thriving town. When he died late in the first century AD, Togidubnus was probably the owner of the palatial villa at Fishbourne outside Chichester (West Sussex), where the main phase of

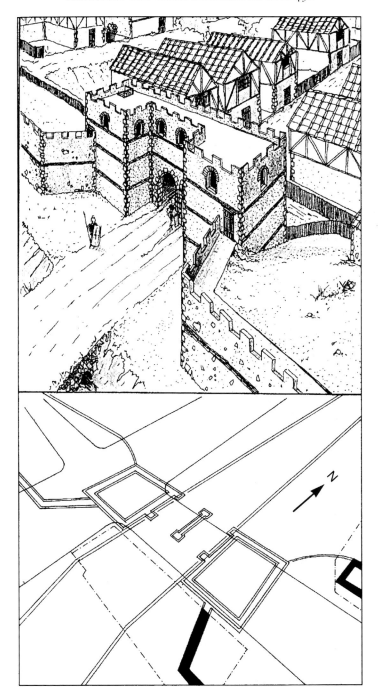

14 Reconstruction and archaeological plan of the South Gate. The plan shows the excavated return wall and latrine. Little is known of the gate itself, apart from observations made in pipe trenches. Note the medieval/ modern site of Southgate Street, further west than its Roman predecessor. The central passage and gate east of the modern road, under St Swithun Street. *After Winchester City Museums; redrawn by Philip Marter*

building is dated to just after AD 70, the centre of a kingdom based around the Solent (Cunliffe 2003, 90). His kingdom may have been inhabited by three different peoples: in the north based on Silchester (Atrebates); in the east based on Chichester (Regnenses), and in the west based on Venta Belgarum (Belgae). On his death a reorganisation of the region occurred: the western element became a *civitas* based on Venta Belgarum and is thought to have stretched westwards toward Bath. This might help to explain the arrival in Winchester of Bath stone found in Roman contexts.

Major building in and around the city followed *civitas* status. An administrative centre was created, based on a forum, which contained shops, offices and a basilica. The orientation of this major building is not known for certain but its site lay north-west of the current cathedral, either north–south across the western end of The Close, or to the south facing the High Street – although a north facing basilica would have been rather dark. Buildings stretched northwards into The Square, where massive foundations have been picked up adjacent to the site of the City Museum. Evidence was recovered in the 1960s and 1980s from the north and south ranges of the offices and shops which bordered the forum: to the south on the Cathedral Green site and to the east at the Wessex Hotel site and north of The Square (see for example WMSN 2, 1988 and *28*). Fragments of masonry have been recovered in excavations, for example part of an inscription which suggests that these building may have been very substantial (*15*). Overall, such evidence as that from the administrative hub of Roman Venta, taken with evidence of the defences (mentioned above) indicates increased significance betokened by major building programmes which developed in and after the final quarter of the first century AD.

For Winchester new status may have triggered civil engineering works. The aim of these works was to extend the city eastwards, perhaps as an open city on that side, on the valley floor of the Itchen. Much archaeological evidence supports this. Excavations in the Brooks in the 1960s and in 1987-8 as well as at Woolworth's in the High Street, have shown that the Romans transformed that area of the valley on which Winchester now stands with drainage channels, and by levelling the area by extending the islands.

To bring this extended platform into being the Itchen was redirected (as the Romans also did, for example, to rivers in Chichester and Cirencester) further to the east to enable the chalk island(s) to be consolidated. Alluvial deposits found both east and west of the Brooks area are not so abundant further east, as was discovered at the Magdalen Almshouses site. Excavations have revealed substantial drainage channels in the Brooks.

THE ROMAN STREET GRID

The axis of the Roman street grid came to be east–west, although evidence from the Brooks excavations may indicate an early north–south road along the island which later had the forum at its south end. The reordering of the city in the late first century possibly involved the extension of the street grid eastwards from the western and central area already established.

15 Fragment 'NTO' of an inscription (?), perhaps from an imperial dedication to one of the Antonine emperors (see Glossary), in which it is set here. It is the largest lettering known from Roman Britain. Found in Middle Brook Street in 1957, its scale – 29cm (11.5in) – might link it to the nearby basilica. *After Winchester City Museums; redrawn by Alejandra Gutiérrez*

The clean yellow/orange surfaces of these streets, swept on behalf of the Roman administration until AD 350, when rough cobbling and patching is found on various sites in the city, not only makes them easily recognisable in the archaeological record, but is a substantial indication of the rise and fall of the Roman administration.

CEMETERIES AND POPULATION

Cemeteries can provide a basis for discussion of population number and ethnicity. It is the exotic that marks out the graves, and this it is often possible to say more about apparent immigrants than locals. From cemeteries, so lacking for the Iron Age, and from other evidence such as distribution of houses, it is possible to speak with some authority about the population of Roman Winchester. By analogy with estimates for other Roman towns of known area, the inhabitants of Venta may have numbered 3-4000 in the second century AD (James 1988, 1-3). This is fewer than the number estimated for the walled area of Winchester in the medieval centuries, but substantial for a Roman town in Britain. Two reasons support this scale of population. First, the Romans did not apparently fill the 550,000sq m of the city, especially in the western area. Second, the Romans created a garden city. Evidence of wide corridors, courtyards and gardens is plain to see in the mid-Roman period, but whether they packed the city more densely in the first and fourth centuries has not been demonstrated.

Roman law demanded that burial should be outside the city walls. Extensive cemeteries have been found north, south east and west of Winchester. From the cemetery north-west of North Gate at Hyde Street and Victoria Road, finds included cremations and burials dating from as early as AD 50 up to *c.*AD 175, some with coins suggestive of soldiers' cash wages. Could these include Romans who occupied conquered Britain in AD 43? The Romans subdued a native population, and the discovery of a horse burial in the bank and pig's head in this extra-mural cemetery hint at native burials and Celtic feasting: natives were obliged to follow Roman burial laws.

The northern graveyard extended for 500m (1640ft): its size suggests that Roman Winchester was populous. At Lankhills, toward its northern extremity, 451 burials were

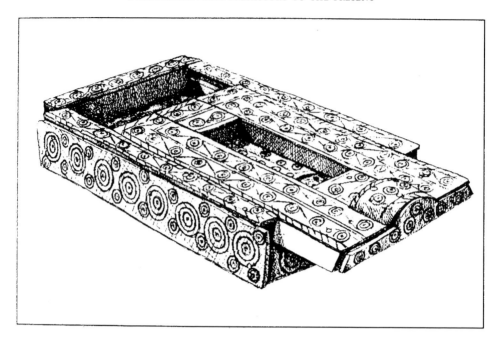

Above: 16 Bone comb box from a fourth-century grave at St Martin's Close (eastern cemetery). The comb in the box was of antler. *Drawn by Judith Dobie; English Heritage*

Left: 17 A costly copper-alloy jug, 15.2cm (6in) in height, from a grave at Grange Road, south of the city, dated AD 85-95. The grave may have been associated with a rural settlement rather than with the city itself, and is among indications of a flourishing villa culture – Roman, or romanised Belgic – in the hinterland of Venta Belgarum soon after the Roman Conquest. *Copyright: Winchester Research Unit*

excavated, almost all dating to *c*.310-410. From the eastern cemetery 110 well-stratified graves were excavated at Chester Road, and a further 40 at St Martin's Close, largely of fourth-century date (*16*). These included an elaborate high-status burial monument over an interment with a lead-lined coffin; such a monument is an unusual find in Winchester.

An element of the southern cemetery has been excavated west of South Gate. To the south-east there were graves at Milland Road, while at Grange Road, rich first-century graves contained bronze and glass vessels, a shale platter and pottery, perhaps relating to a villa rather that to the city (*17*). Elements of a further cemetery or cemeteries have been discovered west of the city. Cemetery evidence suggests some growth in population in the fourth century, and for example at Lankhills, has been adduced to suggest the presence in Winchester of foreigners from beyond the bounds of the empire after *c*.350, precisely the period when the city's phase of Romano-British occupation, characterised by conspicuous consumption, was ending. Isotope analysis of teeth from corpses from Roman cemeteries in Winchester indicate Eastern European and Mediterranean origins: a fourth-century burial of a high-status man in lead coffin excavated outside the north-west corner of the city had, on the evidence of his teeth, grown up in Spain or Italy, and had spent his adult life in Britain (www.winchestermuseums.org, 2006). Before the boon of isotope analysis, the origins of the graves of foreign men and women, both mature and young, were traditionally identified by grave-goods, which included ornaments, brooches and beads as well as evidence of male and female activity – warriors' knives and belt-buckles or spindle-whorls.

Grave-goods associated with incomers have been used to show integration, for their adornments were increasingly British (better quality than those from their native region), and their individual grave practices came to resemble those of natives. The origins of some of these people who were buried at Lankhills have been proposed as the eastern Danube region in Hungary, beyond the imperial frontier, perhaps the area occupied by the Sarmatians. Such foreigners are likely to have come to the city as officials and soldiers, perhaps in a protective role connected with a *gynaecaeum,* or imperial workshop, which perhaps produced clothes for Roman troops in Britain and Germany. A *gynaecaeum* is known from a documentary source at 'Venta', perhaps Venta Belgarum, and unusual water-gates, to allow water build up inside the city walls to be released, were offered – along with Roman baths – as a potential interpretation of a site on the eastern walls of the city (WMSN 26, 1996).

Between 390 and 410 a further group of foreigners, identified from grave-goods as 'Saxons', appears. This is arguably the earliest group of Saxon graves identified in England, showing artefactual associations not only with north Germany, but also with the Upper Thames valley, around Dorchester which, with Winchester, was to play a significant role in the subsequent development of early Wessex. As is often the case in archaeology, voices have been persuasively raised against the immigrant theory, for it can be argued – isotopes aside – that the original invaders of AD 43 were few in number but quickly aped in dress and culture by natives (like the Norman invaders later, see below p.65) and that at the end of the Roman period (*c*.400) the Saxons, not necessarily very numerous, brought new fashions to the Romano-British natives. A group with Saxon affiliations may have been connected with a later fourth-century official or military structure found in the south-east of the city at Wolvesey and paralleled at Dorchester-on-Thames.

SOCIETY AND HOUSING

From the mid-first to the mid-fourth century there is evidence of spacious Roman town houses with roofs covered with stone or tile, stone and rubble walls, and mosaic floors, underlaid by hypocaust heating systems (*colour plate 2*). These houses had painted walls and glazed windows, features shared with rural villas which spring up in the countryside after AD 43, and which have been excavated, for example at Sparsholt and Twyford.

In Winchester there were timber dwellings such as that of second-century date whose burnt out remains accompanied by fragments of plaster were excavated in Staple Gardens (WMNS 2, 1988). Some had wings, around a central garden or courtyard; there were double-corridor-type houses constructed of timber over a masonry base – occupied in the third century; a porticoed house of early fourth-century date with mosaic floors, hypocausts and a stone-tiled roof, and an impressive courtyard house, perhaps with a colonnaded courtyard and mosaic floors, of the fourth century (*18*). Roman tile, for example from hypocaust flues, and brick are found in Winchester, and may have provided the material ground up centuries later to give the plaster in the Saxon Old Minster and in William the Conqueror's palace chapel its characteristic pink tinge. Substantial houses were found at the Brooks, although no one house had all the features listed above and there were variations in quality. The great floral pavements found in insula XXIII house 1 appear to have been of late second-century date and of the highest quality. It was not the first mosaic in Winchester, for black and white mosaics are known from the late first century and later at Wolvesey, Lower Brook Street and elsewhere. The pavements in house XXXIII.3 on the Brooks were considerably later in date than XXXIII.1 and are less artistically accomplished. Altogether fragments of more than a dozen pavements are known in Roman Winchester.

There is increasing evidence of a varied population from the early Roman period onwards. Agricultural activity has been identified on the Brooks island from the first century, with slight timber structures interspersed between layers of cultivation material. Large private residences either side of the street in the Brooks were certainly in existence after AD 150 and may have been built earlier. The Romano-British elite developed an interest in urban living in second-century Venta Belgarum, as at Verulamium and Silchester, and their town houses remained in use throughout the third century.

The fourth century saw these second- and third-century dwellings replaced at the Brooks by a house whose dimensions have been compared favourably with the most opulent houses in Silchester. However, the late fourth century saw the decay, demolition and adaptation of Winchester's great houses. Mosaics were roughly patched, a hearth created in a corridor, and layers of slag and charcoal confirm industrial activity. Some house sites were abandoned altogether, reduced to stub walls projecting above a layer of

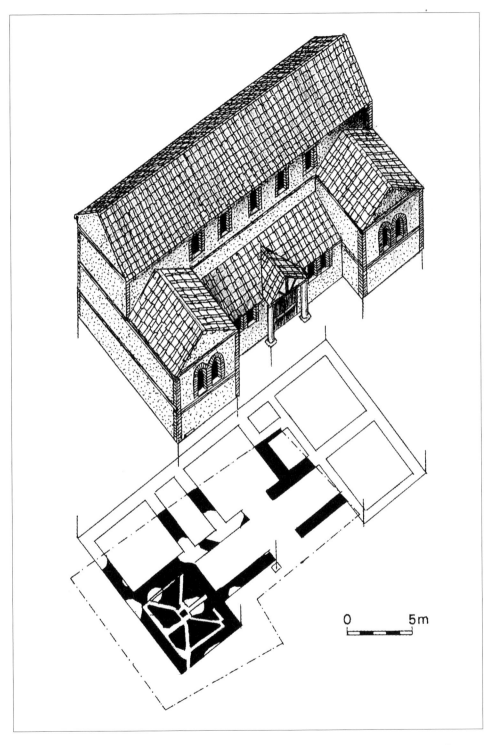

18 Archaeological plan and reconstruction of a spacious Roman house (insula XXIII.3: see Glossary) of *c.*AD 300. The comfortable, porticoed house contained a hypocaust, with its stokehole (left). *After Winchester Archaeology Office; redrawn by Philip Marter*

dark earth which began to accumulate around AD 400. Clearly there was a steep decline in the economic and social status of those who lived in this area of Venta, and it seems likely that this may have been true of the city as a whole.

RELIGION

An indication of early Roman religion at Winchester was a small 'Romano-Celtic temple' of contemporary date with the forum, c.AD 100. Both were found on the tufa island in the Itchen, the temple at Lower Brook Street. A wooden figure of a goddess, possibly Epona, or a worshipper, was recovered from this area of excavation (*19*). An altar found in 1854 in Jewry Street, is inscribed to Italian, German, Gallic and British mother-goddesses (*matres*), and is likely to be of early second-century date. Antonius Lucretianus, seconded for duty by the provincial governor, is mentioned on it as sponsor. He is unlikely to have been a native, and the altar was doubtless associated with soldiers.

The excavation of graves of a significant number of people at the Lankhills cemetery provided an opportunity for an examination of religious practices associated with the dead. Graves were largely from the fourth century, which was a time of transition from paganism to Christianity in Britain: both Christian and pagan graves were excavated. Up to c.AD 350 comparatively little account was taken of the ultimate destination and ease of passage of those who died, although provisions for the journey and some vessels were provided. As the century progressed more valuable offerings were placed in the graves, which indicate observance of rituals and emphasises belief in an afterlife. The evidence of the man with the Mediterranean/British dentition, referred to above, highlights this complex period. In his hand was a coin of the first Christian Emperor Constantine, so was he a Christian? Or was the coin the traditional payment of the pagan worshipper to the boatman over the Styx? Or did the coin betoken an official status for this man?

Further north, ornate combs, such as a beautiful antler comb, its ends decorated with stylised horses' heads, came from a grave at Hyde. Provision of money was again perhaps to pay the mythical ferryman. However, this evidence from Lankhills was not matched by finds at the Victoria Road part of the same cemetery – although probably later than Lankhills – where there were virtually no grave-goods, a situation mirrored at Chester Road in the eastern cemetery. Such discoveries hint at different status or beliefs among those buried in the city's cemeteries. However, dating is not precise and may be a factor in the distinctive evidence.

Because of the early fourth-century date of many of the graves at Lankhills, the overwhelming alignment of the graves with the head to the west could just as likely be a result of the influence of the sun cult (*Sol Invictus*) on late Roman religions, as of Christianity. Among the few gems found in Winchester is a glass one showing a bust of Sol. However, grave-goods such as a platter with a possible chi-rho motif on it could be evidence for Christianity c.AD 330-50. In this case the Christian artefact seems to be associated with a group of graves, perhaps those of a family group, distinct from the general burials at Lankhills. These are early dates for Christian evidence, for Constantine died in AD 337. From very

19 The Romano-Celtic goddess Epona, or a worshipper, displaying a characteristic *mappa* (napkin) and key. Statuette in common oak from Britain or Gaul, 18cm (7in) in height, *c*.AD 150-275. Found in a well at Lower Brook Street 18m (59ft) south of a Romano-Celtic temple of soon after AD 100. *Copyright Winchester Research Unit*

much the same period, the earlier fourth century, a chi–rho monogram was found on a tile built into the corner of the hypocaust in house XXIII.3 at the Brooks (see *18*). However, less than 2m separated this tile from two jars containing animal bone, fish bone, egg shell and mussel shells, apparently placed in the new hypocaust as a pagan offering.

Paganism was a powerful force in Roman Britain, and may have become still more firmly entrenched *c*.AD 350-400 as political circumstances became more uncertain. From *c*.400 a striking piece of evidence for paganism was found in a complex grave at Lankhills where evidence of a stout wooden coffin with male skeleton, remains of a large dog with its legs in the air, a second dog, dismembered, and five bronze coins, not to mention the burial of a decapitated young man with a coin in his mouth were excavated from the same grave. Cremations of the same date were undoubtedly pagan. Decapitations, of which there were several, from the period after *c*.350, might have been punishment for criminals, but those of a two-year-old child and of old women – not otherwise found in the cemetery – carried out *post mortem*, could have been connected with liberation of the soul. Finally, burials petered out in the early fifth century, following a descent into disorder from orderly alignment of the Lankhills graves, while the latest graves at Victoria Road were shallow and more haphazard in position than previously. A pagan cemetery, or cemeteries of fifth- to seventh-century date have been found atop St Giles Hill, in a very prominent and visible position (eg. WMNS Year Review 2000).

POTTERY AND OTHER ARTEFACTS

From the period of the invasion, until the late fourth century, there is continuity of occupation in Winchester, evidenced and dated by a full coin-sequence, and supported by a sequence of diverse pottery types. Occupation evidence begins in the reign of Claudius (died AD 54) with a mixture of imported samian ware from Gaul, and other imported pottery including jars and jugs, mixed with comparatively coarse native wares, which included jars.

What appears, from the quantity and distribution of the vessels found together, to have been the contents of a samian ware shop of the mid-second century, was excavated at the International Stores site on the north side of the High Street. The first-century mixture of imported wares such as the samian, found in the rich Flavian graves south of the city, and very localised pottery, gives way to a more diverse type-series by the third and fourth centuries; New Forest and Oxford pottery is found in the city together with a widely distributed coarse tempered ware of unknown origin. Fragments of glassware also appear, including bases of stemmed glasses suggestive of wine drinking. Trade networks encouraged exchange and brought wealth.

DECLINE

Perhaps before AD 300, and certainly after *c*.350 grand buildings were being demolished and fragments such as a section from a mighty stone column and a moulded stone bracket from the façade of a substantial building were found in a well, filled in around AD 300, together with other high-status objects such as a pewter jug. All the known Roman town houses, numbering more than a dozen, go out of use at this period. An increase in the burials in the Winchester cemeteries after AD 350 was accompanied by a shift in the nature of the settlement away from large stone buildings towards more flimsy wooden ones. The focus of occupation may have changed from within the walls at that time.

Some elements of the economy of the city possibly continued to flourish, or may have been developed, helping to sustain late Roman Winchester, for example the textile workshop (p.39), which may have existed c.350, supplied with wool from sheep on the downland around the city. The bulk of evidence, however, points to problems in the city by the middle of the fourth century.

In addition, the full coin-sequence in parts of the city breaks down: whereas certain sites north and west of the High Street produced fewer coins, elsewhere the sequence of the late fourth and fifth century, coinage continues. This suggests that some sites ceased to be occupied around AD 370, although this may have been a result of changing foci of activity.

THE END OF ROMAN WINCHESTER

Flickerings of urban existence in Winchester continued perhaps until AD 400. Archaeology shows clearly that the city of the second and third centuries underwent comprehensive change. On many sites the period following the Roman occupation is sealed by a black clayey soil usually 15cm (6in) thick but sometimes up to 0.7m (2ft), containing sherds of broken Roman pottery, and indicating that vegetation covered the remains of Roman buildings for a very considerable period. It is doubtful that this 'dark earth' constitutes agricultural layers, for many Roman structures demonstrably protruded through it, although horticulture remains a possibility. Recent research has suggested that it may be possible to identify layers in this dark earth, and that its existence may represent material built up as a result of human occupation, no doubt reduced and of a different type, rather than from complete desertion.

So changed were the functions of the Roman settlement that the street grid was lost for almost half a millennium until c.900, when perhaps only the High Street re-emerged from the Roman plan. However, even this major thoroughfare was differently aligned: further north at least from the centrte of the city, eastwards towards the site of the former Roman bridge over the Itchen and south of the medieval East Gate. The different alignment of Roman and Saxon cross-streets was clearly seen on the Library site in 2006 in the north-west quadrant of the city. Thus the city ceased to show clearly the defining features of town life (see p.27). If the textile *gynaecaeum* closed in AD 407 then this may have been a contributory factor. The transformation of Roman Winchester was exacerbated by the failure of the Roman Empire which prompted adaptation and, as it happened, the collapse of town life at Winchester, and as elsewhere, coincided with the sacking of Rome in the early fifth century. However, links between outlying provinces and Rome were tenuous by the fifth century; and we must look to local conditions for clarification.

What replaced the Winchester of spacious town houses with their mosaic floors and tiled roofs? The few clues there are can be surprising. First, there was the extension of the occupied area of the city, especially in the west, which had not been occupied before with any intensity – in other words, some change of focus. Second, there is the presence of the new feature in the archaeology: extensive evidence of ironworking. Third, the defences were strengthened in more than one place by the addition of bastions. Fourth, there are significantly enlarged cemeteries surrounding the city. Such evidence can be interpreted variously. It could indicate the weakening of imperial bonds and the development of a new military culture in the shell of the old Roman city; or, alternatively, it could indicate a strengthening of connections with Rome with the added military presence and even the establishment of a Roman diocese based in Winchester, c.AD 350-500. It has been suggested that some later Winchester cemeteries became foci for burials from rural communities, maybe giving the crumbling city the air of a necropolis, and masking decline in population size at Winchester. Yet another interpretation proposes the onset of a major plague which decimated the population at this time, the so-called 'plague of Justinian', who ruled for nearly 50 years from AD 518. Whatever the driving forces behind changes in the city at this period, structures were more flimsy, It is possible to suggest the extension of town life in Roman Winchester by half a century or so into the early 440s by use of these military and industrial scraps of evidence.

Even so, the arguments for continuance beyond 400 of 'urban' Winchester are more difficult to sustain, not least because cemetery evidence, our major source for the key indicator – the population concentration – diminishes. There seems to be a 50-year period in the fifth century for which there is remarkably little evidence. Indeed, the rapid dislocation in the pattern, and the decline in the number of burials which had characterised Winchester archaeology throughout the last two centuries of the Roman settlement, signals the end of Roman Winchester. If it was plague that affected the late Roman population of Winchester, and reduced the city's population, then it has a remarkable parallel in the catastrophic decline in the city's population for centuries following the Black Death of 1348-50 (p.96-7).

3

WINTANCEASTER: CONTINUITY AND INVASIONS C.450-1066

SAXON WINCHESTER

Roman order gave way to ruin and desolation and the low-lying, western area of the city reverted to marshland. In Saxon times the Roman name Venta Belgarum gave way to Wintanceaster, The 'ceaster' element in Old English indicates a place recognised by the Saxons as a Roman walled site – the walls were among those Roman features which pierced the 'dark earth'. The survival of the 'Venta' element in the name indicates contact – of an unknown nature – between Saxons and natives, and hints at continuity in some form from the Roman period. However, no dates can be assigned to these contacts between natives and invaders. At the end of the Roman period in Winchester Saxon immigrants came: there is no evidence of Angles or Jutes in the immediate Winchester area. The population of Winchester fell dramatically following the end of Roman Britain: datable material evidence from, for example, cemeteries, falls off, and archaeologists have thus assumed population decrease.

There is sparse fifth-century pagan Saxon pottery from the pits on Lower Brook Street. The focus of Anglo-Saxon settlement is in the Winchester hinterland, for example at Worthy Park where sunken-featured buildings and a cemetery were uncovered: cemeteries begin in the late fifth century, served communities in the hinterland and contain individuals who lived to a good age and were much the same height as people today (WMS 2001b). The pagan Saxons were a rural people who apparently had no experience of life in urban centres such as Winchester. Hinterland Anglo-Saxon survivals could indicate that Winchester continued as a centre of authority, or even as a focus of deliberate settlement by the Saxons, encouraged by a sub-Roman British authority based in the town. However, a map of fifth- and sixth-century archaeological evidence shows little evidence of occupation within the walled city (see *1*). From present evidence there seems to be a break between the Roman and Saxon occupation within the walls: cemeteries in the surrounding area relate to settlements outside the walls (WMS 2001b).

One such may have produced two fragmentary brooches dated *c.*475-525 found near St Catharine's Hill (Stedman 2004).

THE SIXTH CENTURY

The Roman drainage system fell into decay in the two hundred years following the disappearance of Roman urban life after 450. This enabled the River Itchen to reclaim large areas of the eastern part of the city, which had been occupied in the Roman period. The floodplain stretched west of Upper Brook Street, recreating the island on which the minsters were to be built. East of a line from King's Gate to Durn Gate much of the city was probably uninhabitable (WMSN 24, 1996).

This changing environment indicates an authority at Winchester which lacked the resources to keep up an expensive, Roman infrastructure of drainage and massive, stone defences. Thus in the fifth or sixth century the Roman South Gate collapsed, reminding us of the survival of upstanding remains long after the end of Roman power in Britain. However, evidence of military activity continues in the sixth century for military artefacts survive, associated with either attackers or defenders, as exemplified by iron weapons in graves, such as a knife at Winnall and a spearhead from St Giles Hill, both east of the walled area. A further sixth-century cemetery on West Hill lay west of the town (WMS 2001b). Pagan Saxons buried in a concentration of cemeteries outside the city walls in the sixth century may have been the successors of the British natives, or Christian Britons who had reverted to paganism in emulation of the incomers. Cemeteries at Winnall, the first of which has been dated to the sixth or early seventh century, included decapitated burials, such as those found in Roman cemeteries. Such continuity of burial practice could be coincidental, but could, with the discovery of weapons, indicate continuity of military and perhaps administrative urban functions.

THE SEVENTH CENTURY

Traffic continued to lurch over the rubble of the collapsed South Gate until the early seventh century when access at that point was cut off by a ditch. Entry to the city from the south could then have been by the undated King's Gate (as it was known when first documented after the Norman Conquest), which gave access to the site of a royal palace which remains to be discovered archaeologically (p.66). Martin Biddle interprets the centre of power as being, as it had been in Roman Winchester, 'a site in or adjacent to the basilica of the forum, just to the west and north of the present cathedral' within 40m (130ft) of the west front of the seventh-century church. This hypothetical royal site, which probably underlies the western part of the medieval graveyard (where the two war memorials now stand outside the west door of the cathedral – it was not found on the Cathedral Visitors' Centre site), could contribute information to the debate about Winchester in the early Saxon period. At present we cannot be sure of what existed within the walls in the fifth, sixth and early seventh centuries, and when developments took place. However, the authority which restricted access to the city at the South Gate intended to protect something, but what? A palace or royal centre would seem the only option before the return of Christianity.

Conversion of the West Saxons to Christianity followed the arrival of the missionary Birinus in 635. Without royal approval Christianity could not take root. A chapel, only 29m (95ft) long, traditionally founded in the reign of Cenwalh (642-73), became Old Minster. This may initially have been a royal chapel rather than the seat of a bishop. The post-Norman-Conquest text of the *Anglo-Saxon Chronicles* suggests 648 as a foundation date for Old Minster followed by the transfer of the see from Dorchester-on-Thames by Haedda. The appointment 12 years later in 660, of Wine, the first bishop, leaves little time – if the dates are right – for development of an earlier royal chapel after 642.

Archaeology is unlikely to be able to distinguish royal from ecclesiastical work on the Minster site within so narrow a time-frame. It is comparative historical evidence from the Continent which supports the argument for a royal foundation, especially if there was continuity of authority at Winchester from Roman times. The resurgence of Christianity established a religious base which, together with royal status, has remained a key to Winchester's fortunes. Put another way, whereas the Romans were buried outside the cities, Saxons were increasingly to be buried inside the walls.

A clue to how things were being managed toward the end of the seventh century, or in the early eighth century, in Winchester's hinterland came from a high-status warrior burial at Oliver's Battery, south-west of the city, which contained a splendid metal hanging bowl, now in the British Museum. The burial was inserted into a prehistoric earthwork thus showing respect for, and to indicate continuity with, past peoples whose monuments were visible in the landscape. The bowl itself could have been used as a washing vessel, showing respect for, and knowledge of, late-Roman customs, while its origins perhaps in a British area of the West Country suggests a bridging of Saxon and British culture (Barbara Yorke, pers. comm.). All this suggests a preoccupation with continuity of lordship in changing times, but this Saxon authority, perhaps in succession to a residual British authority, built on the perceived power of those whose monuments were left in the landscape around Winchester and in the urban centre itself. In addition to the bowl discovered in the 1930s, a mount from another such bowl was recovered north of Winchester and reported in 1999, adding depth to our scanty knowledge of the area around AD 800. A further cemetery, Winnall II, of the late seventh century, sustains the argument for continuity in the environs of the city.

URBAN ESTATES

Before the relaying of the streets and the creation of the late ninth-century 'burh', at least six estates can be proposed within the town walls from archaeological, topographical and place-name evidence. The royal and ecclesiastical enclosure based on Old Minster and the palace is one, which later in Aethelwold's time (mid-tenth century) became The Close.

Various phases of another compound were excavated at Lower Brook Street. First, a burial dated *c.*650-700 of a Christian female was found. Her necklace denoted high status (*colour plate 3*) and this aristocratic lady may have been associated with the lord of an early Christian estate on which she and others were buried. Apart from the remains of Roman buildings, apparently not in use at the time of the burial, no recognisable structure was found which was contemporary with the burial. By the ninth century on the same site there was a structure, unusually of stone, which produced evidence of gold-working. This building developed into St Mary, Tanner Street, but whether it was founded as a church or chapel, or had other original functions, has not been determined.

Further enclosures are known from documentary sources: at Coitebury, within the north-eastern sector of the Roman walled area (see *36*); at Wulf's Isle (Wolvesey); New Minster and the area bounded by Colebrook Street which was given as an endowment to Nunnaminster. A further estate, Godbegot, is discussed below. The early bishop's residence and its estate from the period before the ninth century, may have been another such compound. The site of this early bishop's palace is predicted by Martin Biddle to have been to the south of Old Minster. Any such structure would be directly beneath the later cathedral.

WINCHESTER AND HAMPSHIRE

As evidence of territorial organisation can be detected in microcosm within the walls of Winchester, so macroscopically it can be seen in the area surrounding the city. In 757 the first reference to Hampshire, the earliest of the shires to be mentioned in a document by name, is found. At first sight, Winchester does not appear to have been central to the establishment of Hampshire, which became the 'county of (South)ampton', drawing on the name of Hamtun, the Saxon settlement at Southampton. This may have referred initially to a Jutish area in the south of the county and the Isle of Wight, perhaps beyond the jurisdiction of the Winchester authority. A centre of power in that area could have been associated with the Roman settlement, Clausentum, on the east bank of the Itchen at Bitterne, which gave way to the thriving Saxon settlement at Southampton: Hamtun, which implies a royal vill and administrative centre, and Hamwic, which suggests a trading settlement.

This place-name evidence by no means proves the precedence of Southampton. Winchester may well have been a focus for the non-Jutish area north of Southampton. In any case, Saxon kings were itinerant and had a number of residences which they used in succession. So Winchester may have been in Saxon times, as today, an administrative centre of the northern area of Hampshire, with a significant royal and ecclesiastical core. It can be argued that Saxon Winchester, like Southampton, took little account of its Roman predecessor, but as in other counties, for example Dorset (Dorchester) and Gloucestershire (Gloucester), the former Roman centres became pre-eminent. The increasing evidence of internal organisation, wealth and population growth within Winchester supports this interpretation.

But such matters are not easily resolved. The question of mints is a point at issue. Coins of Egbert (809-39), for example, have no mint signature so their origin is uncertain. They may have originated at Hamwic, but could have come from Winchester. Unequivocal evidence of a mint in Winchester comes from Alfred's reign (871-99), but the numbers of coins are low, suggesting that minting began at Winchester late in the reign. Mints are not, of course, the only evidence. Pre-Alfredian activity is exemplified in a number of instances and on a number of sites: ironworking (Nunnaminster site) and domestic buildings (The Square and Lower Barracks). Cemetery evidence (Staple Gardens) took the form of some 200 graves possibly of ninth-century date, perhaps, it has been suggested, of immigrants from Southampton after the middle Saxon town was devastated by invaders.

ALFRED, HIS SUCCESSORS AND THE VIKINGS

The Vikings attacked Winchester in 860 and a find of 5000 fragments of mainly stained-window glass may be linked to that destructive raid (WMS 2001b). A Rhenish brooch of the ninth century recovered from the city exemplifies prior links with northern Europe in the age of the Vikings. However, by the reign of Alfred such relations were characterised by warfare as the Vikings attacked inland settlements. In recent years the Vikings have been represented in a more benevolent light than of old, gaining the soubriquet 'long-haired tourists'. But without doubt they were warriors who galvanised the authorities in Wessex into action.

The defences of Winchester were weak by this time and were repaired in the first overall restoration since the fourth century. Not surprisingly such a major undertaking took time: references in West Saxon charters to the exaction of fortress-work first appear in the reign of King Aethelbald (855-60). A remarkable correlation has been shown between the length of the defences in the Burghal Hidage (a document of c.886 in Alfred's reign, when defences were put in order against the Vikings), and the known extent of the Roman walls at Winchester. The existence of ditches from Alfred's time can be shown, but nothing survives of wallwork. For example, upcast from a re-cut ditch, cut by larger pits and dated pottery from the age of Alfred, has been excavated to the west of the city (Sussex Street) as has a ditch to the north (City Road) of the city (see 7). Winchester was the largest of the defended *burhs* (Yorke 1984, 61-70; WMSN 24, 1996).

A start was made on laying out a new street grid by 900 as a secondary activity to the refurbishment of the defences. The new system was in essence unitary, although the excavation at Staple Gardens appeared to reveal the extension of the grid westwards, and that the grid was established in stages. A major task was to recapture the city from the encroaching river flood-plain, and it is believed that the Alfredian street works must have been preceded by the canalisation of the 'brooks' which had flooded eastern areas of the city (WMNS 24, 1996).

This new system of water courses and streets did not generally respect the Roman layout. The High Street was on a slightly different alignment east of the West Gate.

However, recent analysis of work at the Brooks indicates that here was some correlation with the Roman grid on a north–south street excavated in 1987-8. The Saxon grid contained novel features, such as a street running round the inside of the walls to provide easy access to the defences. Streets such as St Swithun Street, within the southern wall of the city still respect the Saxon plan. The Saxon town was organised in plots with a regular perch (20m/66ft) between each street, and with houses increasingly crowded behind the street frontages, gable-end on to the street.

Two street surfaces excavated in the south-west quarter of the city (Assize Courts South) are assuredly of Saxon date. The first was dated by a coin of Alfred (died 899) (1990) and another of Edward the Elder from the early tenth century (1964); the second by a dirham of Samarkand minted in 898. These exciting pre-Norman finds first demonstrated that the street plan, although at this point buried by Norman castle earthworks, was not Roman. The archaeological evidence for the street plan is strengthened by documentary evidence from the foundation charter of New Minster (910) and documented bounds of Nunnaminster written down before 903, by which time they had expanded over earlier boundaries found in archaeology.

Smaller Saxon 'service' streets lay behind the main thoroughfare, such as those now named St George Street and St Clement Street, but the archaeological evidence is not conclusive. Taken together, the evidence suggests a series of works at Winchester lasting well over a century. What is certain in that even before the Norman Conquest elements of this plan were obliterated, notably by the creation, probably in the tenth century, of a new Saxon royal palace nearer to the High Street between The Pentice and Market Street, north-east of the early palace site (see 28).

Such work and expenditure adds up to three things. First, this created a 'burh' at Winchester, one of a series of such defended sites deployed across Wessex. Second, it made Winchester 'a town again' in the sense that there was more potential for dense population and heterogeneous urban functions other those associated with a royal and ecclesiastical vill. Third, the establishment of a new royal palace overriding the newly-laid street grid, gave impetus to Winchester's late Saxon role as a capital and royal centre.

ALFRED AND EDWARD THE ELDER

Hamo Thornycroft's mighty statue, erected in 1901, made Alfred's presence in the city tangible (20). However, Alfred was not a monarch for whom Winchester was a favourite resort. A single visit in 896, when he had Vikings, from two raiding ships wrecked on the south coast, summarily hanged at Winchester, is recorded in the *Anglo-Saxon Chronicle*. While this represents an understatement of his involvement in Winchester in view of the Burghal Hidage and his work on the defences and streets, it is all the written evidence we have of his physical presence in the city. There is evidence that there were local leaders killed supporting Alfred's war-effort against the Vikings including Beornwulf, 'wic-reeve' of Winchester, and maybe also Wulfred, ealdorman of Hampshire (*Anglo-Saxon Chronicle* sub 896).

20 Alfred as a 'heroic peasant' Christian warrior monarch, scourge of the pagan Vikings, sculpted by Hamo Thornycroft (1901). *Photograph copyright John Crook*

Alfred's association with the foundation of a navy centred on the south coast may imply that there was some special link between Winchester and Southampton, an obvious base for such a force. Alfred was apparently generous to the city for, as late as the twelfth century, there is reference to books, believed to have been the gift of Alfred, which had been in the city for centuries – and which did not survive the destruction and anarchy of Stephen's reign.

Alfred's son, Edward the Elder, also showed a firm commitment to Winchester. Edward strengthened his royal status by the foundation of New Minster, a well-endowed religious house which, with Old Minster, became the burial place for West Saxon kings. On completion of the building works, Alfred's body was removed from its place among previous Saxon kings in Old Minster and reburied beside his wife Ealhswith (died 903), creating the long-term link between the great king and the capital of Wessex. He carried on the mint established by Alfred and until the mint was removed (before 1250), the city was a centre for coin production (p.84). Edward the Elder's son Eadred, who died at Frome in Somerset, was brought home to Winchester for burial at Old Minster. Thus as a royal burial place and with a royal mint and palace, the city's future for the time being was assured.

SAXON ECONOMY: TRADE AND INDUSTRY

The nature of the economic driving force behind Saxon Winchester is not securely identified, but must have been allied to the growing political and religious significance of the city. One element may have been a luxury trade, or development of the wool trade in the middle Saxon period for which there is strong evidence at Hamwic. The wool trade was especially valuable to the economy of Winchester as the religious houses came to rely more and on the profits from their endowed lands in order to expand.

The building and development of Old Minster from the seventh century to the eleventh century represented a long-term local industry, which relied on the supply of materials some of which came from a distance. Any stone, other than local flint or chalk, not reused from Roman remains, must have been brought to the city, for example from Coombe Down near Bath. Limestone fragments were recovered from the robbed-out footing trenches of Old Minster. It appears that the Saxons were using new-quarried Bath stone, both for carved pieces and for other purposes, from the beginnings of work at Old Minster in the middle of the seventh century.

More Coombe Down stone is to be seen in those parts of the cathedral, notably the piers of the south side of the nave, which were built after the demolition of Old Minster, than in the eastern arm of the first part of the new cathedral constructed between 1079 and 1093. This could strengthen the argument that the lower courses of the nave were built out of Bath stone from Old Minster, and would explain the wholesale robbing of stone from the Saxon minster.

Trade, industry and administrative activity require adequate communications. The middle of the ninth century – 859 – is the traditional date assigned of the rebridging of the Itchen under Swithun (see p.60 and *24*). Swithun's bridge, now rebuilt as the City Bridge near the site of East Gate, replaced a lost Roman bridge. The re-establishment of Winchester as a bridging point was significant economically and may have contributed to the subsequent popularity of Swithun as a local saint.

The growing economy led to the expansion of suburbs to accommodate the work-force. Tenth-century material remains include evidence of a thriving western suburb,

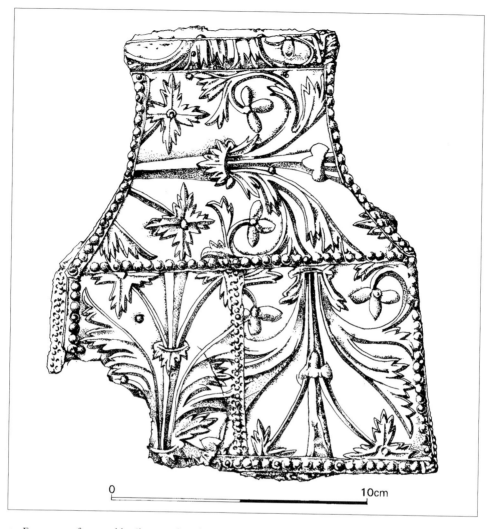

21 Fragment of a portable silver-on-beechwood reliquary recovered from a tenth-century latrine pit in the wealthy western suburb (Sussex Street, 1976). *After Nigel Fradgley; redrawn by Philip Marter*

beyond the defended 'burh' and adjacent to the Iron Age defences (Carfax and Sussex Street). One of this suburb's numerous latrine pits produced a remarkable saint's reliquary (*21*). In the decade before 1066, practitioners of trades were concentrated in particular streets identified by their occupational names.

THREE MINSTERS

Winchester's significance as a religious centre gathered momentum in the centuries following the foundation of Old Minster, which was joined after 900 by New Minster and Nunnaminster. New Minster was placed on land bought with gold by Edward the Elder. It may have been created as a burial place of his father, Alfred. However, its spacious proportions (790sq m/8504sq ft; compare 354sq m/3810sq ft for Old Minster at this time) suggest a place of worship for the people. Like Old Minster before Edgar and Aethelwold's reforms after 963, it was staffed by secular clerks.

Nunnaminster, founded adjacent to Old and New Minsters, provided an opportunity for holy women to practise their faith within a cloister. Remains of the church, uncovered by excavations, are displayed in Abbey Passage beside the Guildhall. Nunnaminster was built on land which belonged to Alfred's Mercian wife Ealhswith (died 903): its boundaries were written into a prayer book of *c*.900, whose Mercian origins link it to her. Edward the Elder's daughter Eadburh, who later was beatified, entered Nunnaminster as an infant; excavations there have uncovered what appear to be remains of a shrine to the local West Saxon saint (see *61*).

These three great churches have been partly excavated and researched by the Winchester Research Unit and the Winchester Museums Archaeology Section. The most extensive excavations were of Old Minster in the 1960s. As a result, the outlines of Old Minster are now marked out, and a complex series of phases of development is explained by information boards, north-west of the cathedral (*22*). In addition, a computer model has been produced in which the viewer cane enjoy a video simulation of both interior and exterior views of this great church, exploring the sight-lines of the kings from their seats at the west end. Associated finds have thrown light on its structure and décor, which in later phases included glazed pottery and relief-tiles used as borders for important areas, and blue glass, some fragments perhaps dating back to the seventh-century church.

High-status works at the minsters – decoration such as mural painting, and fittings such as the organ in New Minster, which is illustrated in a manuscript – are matched by the quality of the architecture, such as the magnificent westworks of the Old Minster and New Minster (see *25*). There is no reason to doubt that Nunnaminster was also a splendid structure, as excavated fragments of the Saxon church have revealed.

TENTH-CENTURY REFORM

A mixture of local, national and international considerations strengthened religious developments in the tenth century. The international component was the reformation of religious communities in western Christendom after 950. In Wessex this was achieved, not without serious opposition, by King Edgar and Bishop Aethelwold (bishop 963-984), who was born in Winchester and is the first named person known to have been born in the city.

The reforms took concrete form in Winchester with the replacement by monks of the clerks who were driven from the Old and New Minsters and the diocese because they 'would not observe any rule' (*Anglo-Saxon Chronicle* sub 963). Benefits flowed from this change: not least that the communal monks were much more cost-effective than the clerks they replaced, and so they were thought to be a better investment and thus

22 Plan of Old Minster laid out beside the present cathedral. The seventh-century cruciform structure (below, *23a*) is outlined in darker brick (centre). The location of Swithun's tomb is seen (top), where the cathedral nave and the minster plan converge (below, *23c*). *Photograph: John Crook*

more pleasing to God, which encouraged benefactors to give. King Edgar led the way in endowing the monasteries. He returned three major estates at Taunton (Somerset), Downton (Wiltshire) and Alresford (Hampshire) together with five other manors to Bishop Aethelwold, in all some 500 hides. Landed income and gifts enabled the startling structures of the rebuilt Old Minster. Ecclesiastical Winchester influenced the Old English kingdom right up to the Norman Conquest.

So it was that King Edgar and Bishop Aethelwold laid the foundations of the wealth of the Winchester diocese. The lands which passed from Edgar to Aethelwold formed the basis of the landed income which made Winchester the wealthiest see in England throughout the Middle Ages, wealthier even than the archbishopric of Canterbury, which Winchester was to challenge for the right to be an archiepiscopal see. The substitution of monks for clerks at the minsters, coupled with the generosity to the bishop by Edgar, was at the expense of dispossessed men of substance: high-born clerks and lay thegns. Some lost their manors in the endowment of the minster, other lay people had their houses demolished in the settling of boundaries between Old and New Minster. Such tensions may have contributed to the murder of Edward the Martyr in Wessex in 978, and to continuing instability in Wessex through to 1066.

SWITHUN

Political instability fuelled a continuing growth in Church power. A final element in the reordering of religious life and experience in Winchester came in 971 with the revelation of the ninth-century bishop Swithun's powers through a series of miracles. In 974 the saint's remains were relocated and given pride of place in the new buildings of Old Minster. Wulfstan Cantor, an eyewitness, recorded that it poured with rain during the ceremony, which is thought to be the origin of the saying which relates rain on Swithun's day to rain for 40 days afterwards (Lapidge 2003).

The discovery and/or rediscovery of saints' remains was an especially English feature of tenth-century reformed monasticism. Also, New Minster already boasted the remains of Alfred and of other kings at this time. The question must be asked: why was Swithun selected as patron of Winchester? Why not Birinus, apostle of Wessex; Haedda, who had translated the see of Winchester, or Beornstan, whose sanctity was the subject of a special revelation to Aethelwold?

One answer is rather mundane. According to Wulfstan, Swithun was chosen because there was general ignorance of him. In some respects ignorance persists, for example in relation to Swithun's death which occurred in the period 861 to 863, though we do not know precisely when. This uncertainty is expressed in citing the date as 861x3. Excavation has shown that Swithun's burial was just outside the original western entrance of Old Minster, as can be deduced from the reconstruction of Old Minster's ruins (23c). Because Swithun was there, the area became a precinct reserved for 'the noble and distinguished'. It can thus be argued that Wulfstan was being disingenuous. Swithun must surely have been known to the monks of Old Minster.

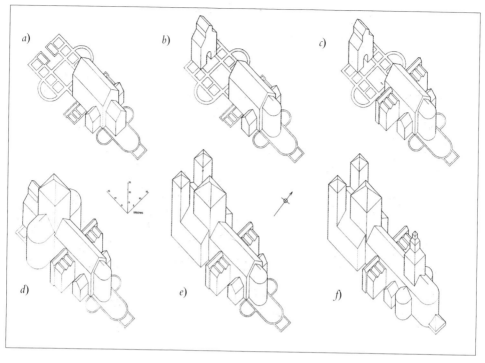

23 Old Minster: structural development, *c.*648-*c.*993-4. The seventh-century chapel developed westwards to incorporate the tomb of Swithun (see *c* and *d*), which remained a shrine-site until the Reformation, covered by a small chapel which protected it. *Copyright Winchester Research Unit*

It is perhaps plausible to suggest that Swithun was 'promoted' a century after his death because a re-evaluation of his life had much to commend it. Swithun had not been a monk as the occupants of the reformed minsters were. He had been a clerk, whose successors had been ejected and excluded in the Aethelwoldian reforms. His resuscitation therefore had all sorts of potential benefits. He was local, saintly and non-monastic, so he could be paraded to bridge the gap between the recently imposed monks and the more substantial clerks who had preceded them in the minsters, and whose departure was causing such friction. Last but not least, Swithun was remembered as having the common touch, as revealed in the miracle at East Gate where he saved the eggs (*24*). The beatification of Swithun was by no means a fraud but it does have the hallmarks of necessity being the mother of invention.

By 980 some of the protagonists were changing and maybe royal interest in Winchester had begun to fade as the fierce yet saintly Aethelwold presided over a more rigorous religious observance. Aethelwold's reforms had been carried through with the royal support of Edgar, who had died in 975 and had not been laid to rest at Winchester but was buried at Glastonbury (Somerset) (Fryde, *et al.*, 1986, 25). King Aethelred, was unexpectedly thrust into prominence by his half-brother Edward's murder in 978. Edward's final resting place was Shaftesbury (Dorset) and Aethelred's London in 1016: the Winchester mausoleum was not filling as Edward the Elder had hoped.

24 The miracle in which St Swithun (left) restores the broken eggs of a poor woman. Swithun was associated with the re-bridging of the Itchen outside Eastgate, and the scene may represent a scene from the opening of the bridge, when eggs were jostled from the woman's grasp in the crush and were dropped as she crossed to market, the great new opportunity provided by a new bridge after centuries without dry passage. *Corhampton Church; photograph John Crook*

However, the rededication of Old Minster on 29 October 980 provided an opportunity for the bishop and the king to reunite at Winchester. Various elements were brought together by this important event in the city's history. The monastic direction in which the reformed minster had been set by Aethelwold was confirmed. Continuing royal interest was reflected in the ceremonial westwork of the new building, which has been shown to have continental parallels, especially in Germany. Inside the building, Aethelred processed to a special throne to receive ecclesiastical blessing. This ceremony was undoubtedly significant in reinforcing Winchester's active rather than passive royal and ecclesiastical pre-eminence in Wessex.

At about this time, the date is not precisely known though was probably before 980, the bishop's complex at Wolvesey was created, replacing that which is believed to lie beneath the present cathedral. Wolvesey probably included a hall (which continued in use until the early twelfth century) and residential accommodation. There was also a curious oval structure which may have been a chapel, a structure matched to the north of the cathedral on the Wessex Hotel site, formerly the New Minster cemetery. The development of Wolvesey completed the occupation of the south-east quarter of the city by rich ecclesiastical buildings, foreshadowing Winchester's long future as a primarily ecclesiastical centre.

LATE SAXON TRIUMPH

The last two centuries of Saxon Winchester, which ended with the Norman Conquest in 1066, were dominated by building at the minsters (25). Provision of masonry, window-glass, bells and the famous organ all support this picture. A walrus-ivory panel dated from 950-1000, representing flying angels set in the gabled roof of a miniature house-shaped shrine was found at St Cross, and is now on display the City Museum (www.winchestermuseums.org, 2006). This is a fine example of late-Saxon carving and can be compared with figure drawings in contemporary illuminated manuscripts and paintings in full-scale architectural settings, such as the angels to be seen at Nether Wallop church (Hampshire). Metalwork and ivory found in excavation constitute the output of a Winchester School of manuscript and plastic arts.

All this demonstrates the high status of late Saxon Winchester. Compared with the local grass-tempered ware characteristic of the local economy up to the eighth century, 'sandy' and 'Winchester' ware are now found. Winchester ware is wheel-made pottery of high quality, but was not widely distributed beyond Winchester so far as current knowledge admits (26). Its high quality echoes the high status of the city at the time, and the sandy-coloured clay is not local, its supply adding to indications of external trade at that time. The Brooks excavation of 1987-8 produced thousands of fragments of Saxon glass. These finds were highly unusual both in their quantity, manufacture and their context, and matched material from Old Minster. The discovery of two Byzantine lead seals, a silver-gilt repoussé head (that is, beaten into relief from the inside) and an Egyptian alabaster vessel in late Saxon layers, leave no doubt about the extended links of the populous and flourishing city at the end of the Saxon period.

Above: 25 Reconstructions of New Minster (left) and the westworks of Old Minster, covering Swithun's tomb, from the north-west in their most magnificent form *c.*993-4-1093. *Copyright Winchester Research Unit*

Left: 26 A Winchester ware glazed spouted ceramic jug, 25.3cm (10in) in height, rim diameter 12cm (5in), excavated at the Brooks in 1987-8. This pottery is found from *c.*950 up to the twelfth century. *Photograph John Crook; copyright Winchester City Museums*

Opposite: 27 A rare Scandinavian burial at the Cathedral Green, perhaps from the time of Cnut (died 1035), of a man aged approximately 23. The inscription translates: 'Here lies G[un]n[i], Eorl's [or the Earl's] fellow.' Note the hand-of-God footstone. *Copyright Winchester Research Unit*

The period of rather less than a century which separates the rededication of the Old Minster from the Norman Conquest and the beginnings of the new cathedral, culminated in a high point of Winchester's development as a capital city, especially when the great, some would say the greatest pre-Norman king of England, Cnut (died 1035), not only chose Winchester as his capital but was also buried there. Scandinavian influence comes to the fore from this reign, as exemplified in the Gunni tombstone (*27*) and a Scandinavian runestone found in the city, but Cnut also emphasised continuity by issuing traditional coinage in his name from the Winchester mint. Given Cnut's status, the comparative lack of Scandinavian finds in and around Winchester is surprising although Scandinavian names were certainly in evidence (see below). The find of a strap-end characteristic of Cnut's time depicting an animal grasping another's head in its jaws is a reminder of the fierce side of Scandinavian lords and their art (WMNS 34, 1999).

The Church continued to benefit from its symbiotic relationship with the crown. The estate north of the High Street, known as Godbegot, a name preserved today for the fine courtyard house on part of the former estate, was given to Queen Emma by Aethelred II in 1012. On her death it was bequeathed to the Old Minster (cathedral priory) and remained the priory's property until 1541. The Godbegot estate in Saxon times was more extensive than it was in later periods, and included a 'fair church' erected by a prefect of the city named Ethelwine, dedicated to St Peter. Remains of this church were excavated in the 1950s when a stone chancel was discovered (now marked on the paving in St George Street), but no evidence of a nave was found by excavation. Numbers of other

Saxon churches are known in Winchester, such as St Mary in Tanner Street and Saxon gate-churches at exits form the city.

The largest landowners were, on retrospective evidence found in the twelfth-century Winton Domesday, the bishop, the prior (ie the head of Old Minster), the abbot of New Minster and the abbess of St Mary (Nunnaminster). The king was lord of the whole borough and was rewarded with ground-rent (landgable). The city's architectural heritage and archaeology at this period show that it enjoyed an impressively broad range of activities, including clothworking, tanning and metalworking, which mark out significant urban communities from their lesser counterparts.

Optimism arising from lay and ecclesiastical reconciliation and the rededication of Old Minster in 980 was apparently well founded. None the less little over a century later Old Minster was to be sacrified by the Normans to their mighty cathedral church. Although the Normans adopted many of the Saxons' best practices (for example the monastic organisation at the minster/cathedral), they destroyed the Saxon royal line and the Old Minster which had existed for over 400 years. Along with the minsters, the buildings of Saxon Winchester have been obliterated by succeeding generations, but much of the Saxon street system still survives and with it numbers of individual house plots and certain urban estates and place-names.

Analysis of the population of late Saxon Winchester buttresses understanding of the significance of Saxon Winchester. Retrospective material in twelfth-century surveys reveals that the population of Winchester in c.1057 (dated by names of moneyers living in the city at that date) lived in 1130 tenements and may have numbered 5500. A higher figure of 8000 is implied by a different method of calculation. The figure of 8000 represents a population of Winchester larger than any between the Black Death of 1348 and the 1820s. The importance of Saxon Winchester is further confirmed by mint evidence which places the city perhaps fourth in England after London, York and Lincoln.

A unique insight into Winchester society before the Norman Conquest is provided by an unparalleled study of personal names found in a survey c.1057. Most names were native Old English: at least 50 per cent and perhaps 75 per cent. Between 5 and 10 per cent were continental Germanic, perhaps representing immigrants who had participated in the Norman invasion, from places like Lotharingia in northern Europe. In addition, there is a small but significant number of Scandinavian names representing two groups: Scandinavians who had migrated to Normandy (giving the area its name) and direct migrants from Scandinavia from the time of Cnut.

The end of Saxon England and the eclipse of its capital were as swift as they were surprising. Signs of the increasing importance of London as a royal centre were already visible from the reign of Aethelred II (978-1016), who, significantly, was buried in St Paul's, although his successor Cnut (died 1035) and Harthacnut (1040-2) were interred at Winchester. However, the remarkable excavations of the minsters, the painstaking re-evaluation of Viking and Saxon activities and rulers, and the recognition of Saxon pottery, metalwork, art and architecture, combine today to give substance to the established tradition which describes Saxon Winchester thriving as 'the ancient capital of England'.

4

NORMAN WINCHESTER
1066-1150

CONQUEST

By the end of 1066 Winchester's fate was sealed, for on Christmas Day 1066 William the Conqueror was crowned king not in Wessex but at Westminster. There Edward the Confessor, whose heir William claimed to be, had begun his abbey *c.*1050, and there Edward was buried. Succession was settled at Hastings in October 1066. Winchester acceded gracefully to Duke William in November and opened its gates. Had Winchester closed its gates to him it is uncertain whether he could have conquered it. He certainly could not have taken London.

A rebellion in 1069 drew William's attention to Stigand, Bishop of Winchester, whose family was allegedly involved. At the Easter Council at Winchester in 1070 Stigand was removed both as Bishop of Winchester and as Archbishop of Canterbury. This cleared the way for a new ecclesiastical start in the city and diocese. Great building activities at the castle and palace had already begun to transform the city by 1072, when the castle provided a useful prison for Stigand.

Also in 1072 King William's new chapel at the castle was probably the location of meetings to discuss the issue of the primacy of Canterbury and York as archiepiscopal sees. It is perhaps significant that such a meeting was held in Winchester, on neutral ground so far as the archbishops were concerned. However, it was a meeting at the initiative of the king in his castle, and not one which was in the domain of the clergy down the hill at the minsters.

CASTLE AND ROYAL PALACE

The aftermath of the Norman invasion was not purely destructive at Winchester; at first the Normans enlarged and extended the types of structures which the Saxons had created, such as the minsters and a palace. Winchester had a part to play in Norman England, but never as its capital: William I governed as he moved around the country.

Winchester was controlled from a castle ordered by William I in 1067, within a year of the Conquest, built on the western side of the valley, within the Roman circuit of defences, south of the West Gate (Biddle 2000, 59). This hillside position dominated the city which spread east of the castle down to the Itchen. The Winchester keep of this early date has not been found by excavation. However, the king was secure at Winchester and the treasury remained in the city. Arrangements at Winchester where a royal palace lay beside the cathedral monastery mirrored those being set in place in London at the same time, where a residence was developed beside the monastic complex at Westminster.

In the south-western salient of the defences over four dozen stone and timber houses were demolished or buried in the creation of the castle platform. This artificially levelled-up site surrounded by a Norman keep must have been tremendously impressive. Today, although the keep has long gone, the great flight of steps which runs up beside the law courts to the medieval great hall of the castle gives an impression of the enormous earthwork bank which the construction of a castle platform in that location demanded. Within the hall itself, towards the eastern end, a trapdoor in the floor provides access into a hollowed out area of the former castle mound, where remains of Saxon stone structures may be discerned. At the northern end of the platform a mighty mound of earth was created, revetted by a stone wall, to dominate the western entrance of the city. A keep was created, together with its accompanying buildings.

A royal chapel within the castle enclosure, perhaps the location of the archbishops' meeting of 1072, has been excavated. It was constructed with long-and-short-work quoins characteristic of Saxon building technique (not found in the cathedral begun in 1079). The internal plaster contained crushed tile to give a pink colour similar to the interior of the Old Minster. As the chapel ignores the Saxon street plan, which had been buried at that point, it must be part of the Norman castle works, and indicates an initial continuity with Saxon architectural style.

The Saxon palace (28), adjacent to the northern boundaries of the religious houses, was extended by the Normans. Royal visitors stayed in the palace, which documentary evidence suggests doubled in size around 1070, although there is as yet virtually no archaeological evidence of it, other than a wall excavated in the vicinity of St Lawrence church. The rebuilt palace was splendid, 'second neither in design not size to those at London'. Kitchens are referred to on a site now immediately adjacent to the eastern end of The Pentice, south of the High Street, where twelve houses were destroyed to make room for them (28). Today the projection of structures on the corner of Market Street into the High Street ghost the site of the kitchen (29). William also built a hall and other palace buildings.

These major works, together with those at the cathedral, may have encouraged some of the overseas links of the late eleventh-century Winchester, which are found in the archaeological record: four Byzantine coins and seals (Biddle 1991), and, more prosaically, Andenne pottery from Belgium.

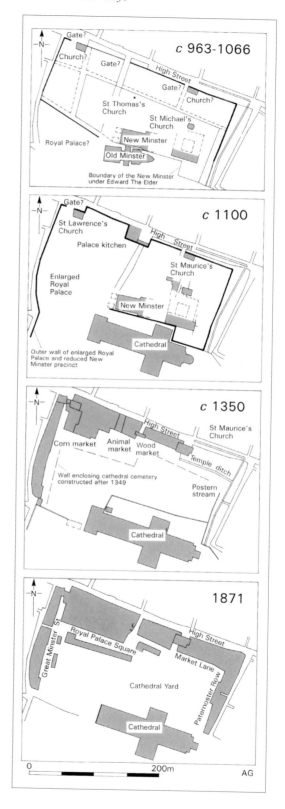

28 Plans of the late Saxon and Norman palace site. The location of the Norman kitchen (the square structure centre top c.1100 and c.1350). The palace buildings lay west of the kitchen under what is now The Pentice and included the site of St Lawrence church. After the Black Death a significant proportion of the graveyard was commandeered by the townspeople, as shown by the dotted line on the plan. The line of that wall is readily traced on the ground today. *After Keene and OS; drawn by Alejandra Gutiérrez*

29 25 High Street, formerly Ratners, projects northwards into the street echoing the encroachment of the long-lost royal palace kitchen across the High Street, narrowing the townspeople's main thoroughfare.
Photograph John Crook

Around 1100 the castle began to combine the functions of residence and fortress, perhaps at the expense of the palace. The castle remained a major treasure house in the reign of Henry I (1100-35), who rode there to secure treasure on the death of his brother, William II (Rufus).

WINCHESTER CATHEDRAL AND NUNNAMINSTER

It was in a city already witnessing two major building projects, at the castle and the palace that work on the cathedral was begun in 1079-80 (*colour plate 4*). By this time the realm was secure and the ecclesiastical hierarchy had been reorganised. The capital of Saxon kings was appropriate for a new, grand building of 'colonial' proportions to leave no doubt that in ecclesiastical matters as in lay, the Saxon age was finished.

On 8 April 1093, 14 years after it was begun, the formal dedication of the east end of the new cathedral took place. The remains of Swithun were removed from Old Minster and set in the eastern arm of the new building in a surprising enthusiasm for a Saxon saint by conquerors generally sceptical of the sanctity of those revered by people they had conquered.

Materials for facing the new cathedral had to be brought from a distance: mainly quarries at Binstead, near Ryde, on the Isle of Wight. The very considerable amounts of material used inside the walls, faced by this ashlar, were local flints. This building, the longest of its kind in Europe at that date, was intended to impress. To imagine

30 The Norman cathedral as projected. The westworks, probably built soon after 1100, were demolished *c.*1350; towers at the corners of the transepts were projected, but internal architecture now shows the plans changed before they were completed. *After John Crook; redrawn by Judith Dobie*

Winchester with its Norman castle, palace and cathedral gives a clear impression of the Church and State in the later eleventh century.

But a view of Winchester with all these projects completed at once would be illusory, because the plans evolved as time passed (*30*), and because different elements were in train at different times. The spectacular length of the cathedral nave is a puzzle, and was late on the scene. The Conqueror had respected Winchester, and his son Rufus supported the cathedral with additional grants of quarry-land on the Isle of Wight. However, the restless lifestyle of William I, visiting lands in France and England, and the predilection of Rufus for court and hunting meant Winchester Cathedral was increasingly a project which had to take its chance. Bishop Walkelin (1070-98) was undoubtedly an ideal choice to set the cathedral and diocese on a new track after the pluralistic Stigand.

Nunnaminster was also reordered by the conquerors and was very popular among the Norman rulers and their families as a religious house for their daughters, who brought new endowments. The dedication to St Eadburh was changed soon after 1066. Excavation of the pier bases has revealed a curious arcade supported on alternate 'cruciform and circular shaped drum columns', which together with the wide bands of mortar found in Walkelin's work on the cathedral, suggests that the reworking of Nunnaminster was well in hand by *c.*1100 and was on a significantly larger scale, almost three times as wide a its Saxon predecessor (WMSN 28, 1997).

DECLINE IN ROYAL STATUS

Rufus (William II, 1087-1100) was not a king whose life recommended him to bishops. Where Rufus had no children and perhaps had an interest in men, Henry I lay at the opposite end of the sexual scale, having possibly two dozen illegitimate children by a variety of mistresses. Perchance the private lives, nepotism and patronage of these two kings contributed in some degree to the division of Church from State at Winchester.

The cathedral tower collapsed in 1107, seven years after Rufus was buried there, the last king to be laid to rest at Winchester (see 32). This collapse, and the major rebuilding which followed, may have contributed to Henry I's break with the Norman tradition, when he abandoned the Easter crown-wearing at Winchester c.1110. The ceremony had become a feature of Norman kingship, presumably after the westworks, probably twin towers, were completed at the cathedral, if that was where it took place. Such a tradition was, therefore, not long standing, and was easily discarded. The growing influence of London was another significant weight in the balance.

Also around 1110 King Henry initiated a survey of Winchester, possibly an updating of the now-lost 1086 Domesday, to try to discover, as his father had done, what encroachments had occurred on royal estates in the city since the time of Edward the Confessor. It would seem likely that such a survey would prove unpopular, and there is evidence of wary answers from the 86 jurors such as 'we know not by whom'.

The year 1110 was significant in another way, for by that time sufficient work had proceeded on the new buildings at Hyde for the monks of New Minster to migrate there, carrying with them the remains of royalty, notably Alfred's members of his family. Relics of St Grimbald and St Judoc were also taken there. The abbey was very large, perhaps among the five largest abbey churches in England, and was built in the height of Romanesque splendour. Capitals now at St Bartholomew Hyde parish church exemplify this quality, and from an early date the church had impressive schemes of stained glass, replaced or enhanced (together with sculptural updating) each century until the Dissolution (Birkbeck and Moore 2004; WMNS 35, 1999). Henry I must have been a significant donor, as he was to the equally splendid Benedictine house at Reading, where his heart is buried. Recent community archaeology has partially unravelled the mystery of the triple burials, marked by slabs, before the former high altar at Hyde. The tradition that these were of Alfred, his wife, and his son Edward the Elder, who had brought the project at New Minster spectacularly forward by 903, has been reinforced by this recent work. Fragments of stone found deep down in the former grave-sites, may have been fragments of the tombs, and coffins. The eastern end of the church is now clearly marked out on the ground, the drum pillars of the church suggested by plantings on the pillar sites. The celebration of the 900th anniversary of the migration to Hyde is eagerly awaited in 2010 (www.winchester.gov.uk for the Community dig; WMNS 35, 1999) (colour plate 5).

31 St Mary by West Gate, chancel arch, now demolished, and West Gate. The position of the twelfth-century arch shows that the chancel must have pierced the city wall, with nave outside the wall. This suggests that the church was built at the time when Henry I's giant outer-bank defences were in progress, which began to encircle the town from the west before 1120. Henry's *enceinte* was never completed, and this church would have been built after construction began. *Author's collection*

Perhaps a symptom of the collapse in Henry's relations with Winchester may be detected in 1118 when one of his treasury staff, Henry the Camerarius, was blinded and castrated for irregularities in treasury affairs. Although the city remained a treasury town thereafter, it was increasingly less significant in that role. However, relations between Henry I and the city were by no means always poor. He acted as go-between in the acquisition of lands for the New Minster when it moved north of the city to Hyde *c.*1110. He continued to take an interest for the following two years at least, acting probably on Bishop Giffard's advice.

The survey of *c.*1110 provides an unrivalled snapshot of the city within half a century of the Conquest. So far as the boundaries of twelfth-century urban Winchester are known they may have been defined by five churches: Winnall (north), St Anastasius (north-west), St James (west), St Giles (east) and St Faith (south). The area of the constituent parts of the city by the late twelfth century, and by an analogy also early in the century, consisted of the walled city of 58ha (144 acres) with a somewhat smaller area of 49ha (122 acres) to the south outside the walls, and three roughly equal suburban areas on the north, east and west, each around 20ha (50 acres). Around the expanded city a substantial outer series of defences was begun under Henry I. These lay outside West Gate and parallel to the ancient defences (*31* and see *36*). The northern section may have been at Clifton Road.

These major works of the early twelfth century were abandoned before completion. The creation and abandonment of such defences signal shifts of royal interest in Winchester. Henry I is known as a builder of defences elsewhere, for example round the town of Argentan in Normandy, and the outer defensive *enceinte* at Winchester resonates with outer defences at Cologne in Germany. Nearer Winchester it has been suggested that Henry I, 'stagfoot' to his contemporaries because of his unrivalled knowledge of stags and hunting, is the likely developer of the giant deerpark at Clarendon (Wiltshire), enclosed by a bank well over 16km long (much longer than that begun at Winchester), where he had created a vast laboratory to pursue his scientific hunting passion (James and Gerrard 2007). The 1110 survey thus reveals the city at the height of its medieval development, with the great building programme and burgeoning population.

POPULATION AND SOCIETY

From perhaps 8000 before the Conquest, the population may have declined in the turmoil immediately after 1066. But in the early twelfth century the city contained perhaps 1300 houses, making it second only to London and larger than both Norwich (1270 houses) and York (1181 houses). Such figures translate into a population of 8-11,000 in the early twelfth century. At the time of the Winton Domesday of 1148, the city population was probably somewhat diminished as a result of civil war. Because of the widespread destruction chronicled in 1141, a figure nearer 8000 might be appropriate for 1148.

Physical changes in the city are clearly mirrored in the changes in composition of the population. Only 30 per cent of those recorded at Winchester in 1110 had native names, compared with 70 per cent in the pre-Conquest survey. While there was a tendency for those with Norman names to be more substantial citizens who had gained from the invasion, and so to be recorded, the tilt in balance of power in the city is striking. In addition, there may have been an especial rise in the numbers of Normans who settled in the royal fief, perhaps one-quarter of the city, to which the survey is restricted. There is, however, no conclusive evidence that the Normans settled in a single area of the city. There is also a significant element in the changes in names which derived from changing fashion; as shown above, many with English and Norse names giving their sons continental or biblical names thus change the appearance on paper, if not necessarily the bloodlines of the city's population. In post-Conquest Winchester we can see the role of fashion in nomenclature, in ways that are hidden from us in previous Roman and Saxon 'invasions' where fashion to match the invaders' appearance may have been significant.

BISHOPS GIFFARD AND BLOIS: WOLVESEY

At first any incipient decline was masked by the building activities of two great bishops: William Giffard (1100-29) and Henry of Blois (1129-71). As Rufus's chancellor, Giffard had been responsible for the cavernous Westminster Hall and was an ideal person

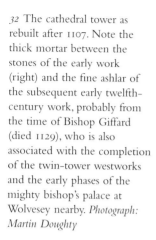

32 The cathedral tower as rebuilt after 1107. Note the thick mortar between the stones of the early work (right) and the fine ashlar of the subsequent early twelfth-century work, probably from the time of Bishop Giffard (died 1129), who is also associated with the completion of the twin-tower westworks and the early phases of the mighty bishop's palace at Wolvesey nearby. *Photograph: Martin Doughty*

to oversee the reconstruction of the collapsed tower and the damaged transepts at Winchester cathedral, where the superlative quality, closely mortared late Romanesque stone work, has Giffard's stamp upon it (*32*).

The development of the bishop's palace at Wolvesey into probably the greatest Romanesque house in England was accomplished during the episcopates of Giffard, who undoubtedly built the West Hall and range, and of Henry of Blois, who built a great East Hall and much else – although it remains possible that Giffard was the originator of both East and West Halls at Wolvesey (*colour plate 6*).

Among the many architectural features of Wolvesey was a water system, which has been traced in the courtyard and under the south range. Its contents enabled the pottery sequence for Winchester to be re-evaluated and types previously dated to the thirteenth century to be moved firmly into the first half of the twelfth century. Wolvesey also reveals much exceptional high-status building work of the twelfth century as exemplified by the fine stonework of the West Hall, which matches the close-mortared late Romanesque work of the rebuilt cathedral tower. The West Hall enjoyed a raised *piano nobile* from which the cathedral monastery could be viewed, and overlooked a terraced garden. Much of Giffard's work is now buried beneath the Baroque palace, but the ruins of the northern end of the west range can be seen.

Giffard's successor Henry of Blois, whose brother Stephen became king of England in 1135, began his episcopate with major building programmes; the complex at Wolvesey was developed magnificently. The impressive ruins which remain today date largely from the twelfth century. A major consolidation programme was undertaken by the custodian, English Heritage, to display the halls, kitchens and many associated buildings. Embellishments, such as fragments of the ornate Caen stone decoration of the doorway of the west range added by Bishop Henry, are in the City Museum (*33*).

33 Caen stone sculpture fragment from Henry of Blois's palatial Wolvesey, the *domus quasi palatium, c.* 1140-50, perhaps from a richly decorated doorway, 15.5cm (6in) in height. Originally polychrome (red eye, black eyebrow and hair), from a high setting as the top of the head remained uncarved. *Copyright Winchester Research Unit*

34 St Cross church from the south-east to show the twelfth-century work. It was traditionally thought that originally the hospital buildings lay south of the church (left of the picture), and that the south side of the church is for that reason more plain architecturally than the north, 'public' side. However, recent geophysical prospection south of the church found no evidence of buildings or of foundation trenches, implying that the original, twelfth-century cloister was superseded on the same site by Beaufort's fifteenth-century rebuilding. *Photograph John Crook*

35 The leper hospital of St Mary Magdalen: site plan and aspects of the buildings. The church was rebuilt in the fourteenth century, but the twelfth-century pillars were preserved. The buildings were demolished in the late eighteenth century. A *Time Team* excavation televised in recent years, undertaken in appalling weather conditions, revealed aspects of the graveyard. *Author's collection*

The mid-1130s were notable for another, now largely vanished, building project initiated by Henry of Blois. This was the Hospital of St Cross, with an impressive Romanesque church, parts of which still survive, and a range of ancillary buildings (34). The now lost leper hospital of St Mary Magdalen, east of the city, is another project attributed to Bishop Henry. Romanesque work was still upstanding in the late eighteenth century (35). Surprisingly, field walking in the 1980s produced no twelfth-century artefacts. However, excavation both on the site of the chapel, the almshouses and in the cemetery by *Time Team* in March 2001, produced evidence of the structures and also uncovered a skeleton with evidence of early-stage leprosy, enabling a reconstruction to be made of his head, now visible on the Channel 4 website (www.channel4.com/history/microsites/T/timeteam/archive/2001win.html).

CIVIL WAR AND ANARCHY

The royal palace appears to have ceased to function by the death of Henry I in 1135. Stephen (1135-54), if he stayed at Winchester, probably used the castle, where the treasure was stored. Stephen's reign was very unsettled and, from the city's point of view, crucial.

In February 1141 Stephen was captured at Lincoln by forces loyal to his rival, the Empress Matilda. His brother, Henry of Blois, no doubt sensing disaster for himself in the wake of Stephen's defeat, handed over the crown and treasure to Matilda at Winchester Castle. This turned out to be a false move for the bishop and was almost fatal for Winchester.

Henry of Blois and Matilda came to blows. Matilda was based at the castle and Henry in the old royal palace in the centre of Winchester (or possibly Wolvesey). In the succeeding battle, areas of the city were devastated and the royal palace destroyed. Although Henry was successful, the price for the city was very high for August and September 1141 Winchester was burnt – some said torched. Apart from the loss of the royal palace, the castle was attacked on all sides, including from within the city, from the Southgate Street area. Quite what the effect on the castle was can only be imagined, but we hear nothing more of it in the remainder of Stephen's reign. To date, little archaeological evidence has been found to endorse the chroniclers' description of the burning of Winchester, although fire damage of the mid-twelfth century, to the south-western part of St Mary's abbey cloister, was uncovered by excavation in 1973 (see *61*).

THE 1148 SURVEY

Henry of Blois was responsible for a survey of lands at Winchester in 1148. The survey reveals the city damaged by civil war (*36*). It is a fuller survey that that of 1110 – perhaps because the bishop was enjoying the benefits not only of his own properties as bishop, but also those of his brother, the king.

The survey suggests a population of approximately 8000 people occupying 1100 houses. Three suburbs, although not that on the east, were heavily populated. The defensive work begun for the western suburb earlier in the century perhaps encouraged the spread of houses into the suburbs. Within the walls the city was well packed with houses, including the High Street frontage of the defunct royal palace where 15 tenements had sprung up since 1141. There were high values attached to properties in the main thoroughfares including those leading to the gates.

Occupations were varied. Royal officials and moneyers dominated town society, but they were neither numerous nor as important individually as they had been 40 years earlier. The moneyers remained in the High Street where they had been since the Conquest, and were joined in the city by both Christian and Jewish goldsmiths and moneylenders. Otherwise, food trades were common while shoemakers and tanners were dispersing from the streets which bore their names.

Winchester must have shared in the general expansion of European trade which culminated in the commercial revolution of the later twelfth century. Set against this speculation, archaeological evidence in the city for outside connections is sparse in the middle and later part of the twelfth century.

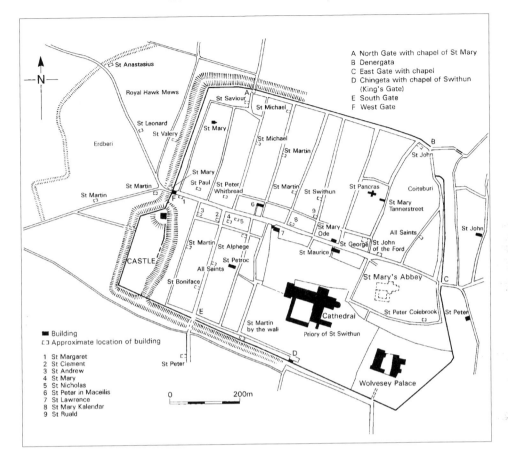

A North Gate with chapel of St Mary
B Denergata
C East Gate with chapel
D Chingeta with chapel of Swithun
   (King's Gate)
E South Gate
F West Gate

■ Building
⊑⊐ Approximate location of building

1 St Margaret
2 St Clement
3 St Andrew
4 St Mary
5 St Nicholas
6 St Peter in Macellis
7 St Lawrence
8 St Mary Kalendar
9 St Ruald

0   200m

36 Winchester in 1148. Much of the Saxon street plan is clearly seen and the gates are identified. Water courses in Upper Brook Street (Sildwortenestret), Middle Brook Street (Wunegrestret) and Tannerestret (Lower Brook Street), may have contributed to the stabilising of the watertable by the tenth century, which allowed the creation of a dry crypt for the cathedral. many of the 50 or so churches of medieval Winchester are located on this map. Castle, cathedral and Wolvesey Palace are seen in their Romanesque plan. The massive earthwork outer defences west of the city, construction of which was abandoned by this date, are noteworthy. *After Winchester Research Unit; redrawn by Alejandra Gutiérrez*

PARISH CHURCHES

The study of parish churches provides a barometer of the fortunes of the city in the Middle Ages: their number and development hint at general trends of boom or decline. Within the city the number of parish churches peaked at some 57 by 1148 (see *36*). Thereafter, reduced numbers were probably due to the decline of the city and to developments which flowed from the investiture contest of the eleventh and early twelfth centuries. In this battle of Church and State, the Church discouraged lay people from developing private churches, the origin of many churches in Winchester. When Salisbury was founded after 1220, it had just three churches – facilitating administration, and with much larger and so more viable parishes than those at Winchester, which were estimated at the height of the church boom to have covered no more than 1.1ha (2.8 acres) per parish. The clergy formed the largest occupational group at Winchester in 1148. While their buildings no doubt needed maintenance, the unproductive nature of clerkly life boded ill for the future economy of the city. Evidence of parish churches taken with other materials from the 1148 survey suggest that Winchester may have been maintaining a position among the top six cities of England towards the end of Stephen's reign, but it is difficult to be certain.

Summing up, there is more documentary evidence than for earlier periods, and it tells us much. But there are significant gaps: stylistically and using narrative sources we can attribute buildings to men such as Giffard and de Blois. But there are few administrative accounts until after 1150 for royalty (so we know little of Henry I and virtually nothing of Stephen's reign, who if he had anything in common with his builder-brother Henry of Blois, must have made a contribution) and nothing before 1200 for the bishops. On the archaeological side there is a comparative dearth at present of domestic material and we have no published pottery sequence, although much evidence survives from the great buildings – cathedral, castle and Wolvesey Palace. The first stone domestic accommodation of the townspeople begins to survive above-ground, notably at 24 St Thomas Street where an early twelfth-century hall survives over a two-bayed undercroft. Like two other such properties known in the city at the time, it was set back from the street. At the other end of the archaeological scale, among the novelties in the archaeological record of this period, are flutes made of goose bone, and small bells from clothing or for undefined ecclesiastical functions.

5

RECOVERY 1150-1300

A visitor to Winchester in 1150 would have found the city considerably damaged by the siege of 1141. Nonetheless, the principal structure on the skyline would have been castle with its square Norman keep. Below it was the cathedral, beside which was the Norman royal palace, probably in ruins. Wolvesey would have been approaching its fullest Romanesque extent. These structures dominated the southern half and the margins of the city. Winchester was still under the direction of royal and ecclesiastical authorities, which commanded significant spaces as owners, occupiers or landowners.

This period saw the city flourishing in an age of general economic growth, which is reflected in a variety of ways: in the number of parish churches, the introduction of new religious houses, the friaries, while art and architecture on the grandest scale is plainly seen. On a lesser scale, but still complex, the earliest dated timber-framed house in the city dates from before 1300. The city government developed through grants and charters, and became a property holder in its own right. This was to be significant for the future.

In the city centre, and to the north of the High Street, were the main residential areas. These were served by some 50 parish churches, many of stone, while the housing was predominantly timber-framed, with a small proportion of high-status houses interspersed. Certain streets, for example in the Brooks, were areas of industrial activity, notably textile working. The suburbs were growing.

HENRY OF BLOIS: ST CROSS AND THE WINCHESTER BIBLE

Although Bishop Henry anxiously left England on Henry II's accession in 1154, he was back in 1158 and developed his buildings until is death in 1171. These architectural works share a number of characteristics among which is the use of significant amounts of Purbeck marble. Bishop Henry's interest in Classical antiquity had already led him

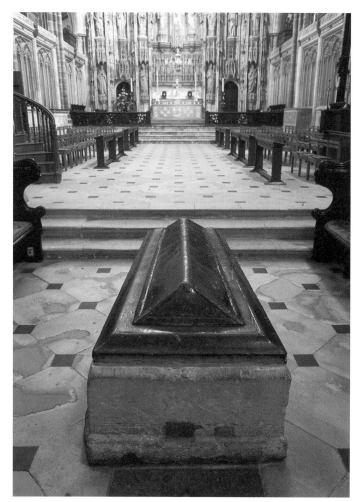

37 The Purbeck marble-topped tomb in the choir of the Cathedral. It is now believed on the grounds of material, style and contents, to contain the remains of Bishop Henry of Blois (died 1171). Bishop Henry was among the greatest sponsors of the twelfth-century renaissance in Winchester and was brother of King Stephen. *John Crook*

to Rome whence he had shipped back *spolia* (see Glossary). It may have been that this excited his interest in marble and led him to seek out suitable materials in England.

Henry of Blois was an innovator in the use of Purbeck marble as his works pre-dated by 30 years or more the 1174 rebuilding of Canterbury Cathedral, a first date commonly given for the extensive use of that material. Hyde Abbey and Bishop's Waltham Palace, as well as Wolvesey and St Cross, all incorporate carved Purbeck. At St Cross there was an early unsuccessful experiment in the chancel of the chapel to make Purbeck load-bearing. The black Purbeck column bases can still be seen protruding below casing columns of limestone. The squared east end of St Cross, in the English style, was a significant triumph. The finely carved late Romanesque decoration of the chancel, both inside and out, is the best of this date in the city.

Henry of Blois made no obvious contribution to the fabric of Winchester Cathedral, apart from the provision of the marble font, from Tournai. His greatest contribution to the cathedral was of another kind: the Winchester Bible (see *colour plate 7*). This extraordinary book, among the greatest achievements of twelfth-century art in Europe, is displayed in the cathedral library. Monumental in concept, the illumination, like the cathedral priory which housed it, was never finished. However, a text was completed, originally bound in two great volumes: each spread measuring 583 by 792mm (23 x 31½in). A revealing fact about the scale of the Bible is that it took the skins of some 250 calves to create the pages. The decorative lettering was achieved by artists whose contributions can be identified and collated. The decoration of the pages contains much gold leaf, but it is the deep blue lapis lazuli fetched from Afghanistan, more valuable than gold, and of which greater quantities were used, that demonstrates the sumptuous nature of the Winchester Bible (Donovan 1993).

The Bible, associated documents, wall paintings, sculpture and other evidence of the Winchester School from the second half of the twelfth century give clear indications of the wealth of a patron such as Henry of Blois. These creations illustrate a range of materials from the workshops of medieval religious artists in the city. The work of the Winchester School is by any standard outstanding and reveals the world of high art at the end of the period of Winchester's pre-eminence as royal and ecclesiastical centre. There were many stately bishops after Henry of Blois, but perhaps not even Peter des Roches (died 1238) or Henry Beaufort (died 1447) had the means that Henry of Blois could call upon from his estates, not only as Bishop of Winchester and Abbot of Glastonbury, but also, until the king's untimely death, as brother of King Stephen. A great age passed with the death of Bishop Henry in 1171.

HENRY II: STABILITY AND INVESTMENT

The accession of Henry II in 1154 brought stability. In 1155 there was evidence in the newly instituted exchequer roll that works were in progress at the castle (38). They were standard entries suggesting that works at Winchester were already a regular feature of Stephen's reign. The exceptional characteristic of the exchequer accounts for Winchester Castle is that here alone, of all castles on the royal roll, did expenditure on houses and chapels within the castle precinct exceed expenditure on defence in the period to 1189. So, either the castle defences were in good condition or, because he lacked the facilities at the palace site which had been put to other uses, the king needed the castle to double as a palace. There is nothing to suggest further works near the cathedral.

Henry ruled from the borders of Scotland to the Pyrenees. It was from Anjou that his dynasty took its name, there its heartlands lay, and it was there at the convent of Fontevrault that he was buried. Royal Winchester was less significant than at any time since the Norman Conquest. Moreover, the Angevin connection tended to favour the development of Southampton.

Henry, an enthusiastic hunter and hawker, conducted business as he travelled. At Winchester he built a birdhouse at the castle in the 1170s and established his 'Hawkheye' outside the walls of the north-west of the city, near the site of the new Hampshire Record Office. Royal huntsmen, hawks and hounds occupied this complex where timber and

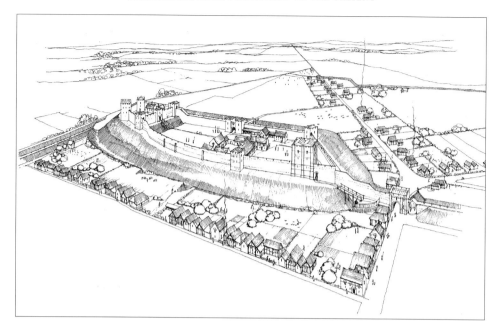

38 Reconstruction of the castle at the time of Henry II (1154-89). Note the square keep and towers. *Drawn by John Reynolds; copyright Hampshire County Council*

stone structures were revealed in excavations in 1985. These excavations revealed the remains of a gyrfalcon, birds known to have been imported by John to the region soon after 1200 while the same area – the western suburb – produced a cornucopia of wild birds from mallard and teal to heron and crane, buzzard and kite, many if not all very likely remains of victims of the royal falcons (WMNS 33, 1999).

On several occasions Henry found himself embroiled in wars against his wife Eleanor and his sons. Perhaps in response to the rebellion of his son 'young Henry', the king carried out defensive works at Winchester Castle in 1173-4. Here Queen Eleanor was imprisoned after her children rebelled. Henry's relations with his family were the subject of an allegorical mural painting in Winchester Castle, depicting an eagle on its nest being attacked by its young. Work in the castle precinct in the 1170s evidenced another failure in Henry II's life: the murder of Archbishop Becket. A chapel dedicated to Becket was created, with another dedicated to the Breton St Judoc whose relics were at Hyde Abbey. A treasury, a gaol and a herb garden were also built (Biddle and Clayre, 2000).

RICHARD I AND JOHN

When Henry II died in 1189, Winchester had already entered a period of eclipse as a capital. Richard (1189-99) had spent most of his life abroad and continued to do so. However, he came to Winchester for a coronation, staying at the castle, from where he made his way to the cathedral. His mother Eleanor watched the coronation from high in the south transept.

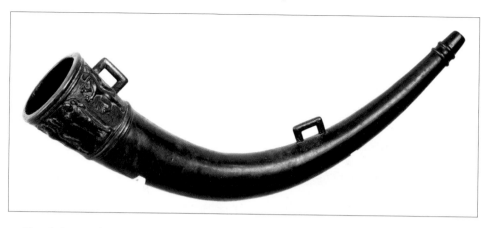

39 The city's moot horn, recorded in documents before 1300 and perhaps twelfth century in origin (suggested by its decorative style). In medieval times it is believed to have been sounded to summon the freemen's assembly, although the earliest museum catalogue record (of 1853) ascribes it to the castle's 'warder'. More recently it was played atop the West Gate in 1927. A replica was made in *c.*1996 which has been played both in city and cathedral settings to match its symbolic decoration. Measurements: (max. diameter) 58.5 x 9.9cm (23 x 4in); weight 6kg (13lb). It is cast in 'leaded gunmetal' and was recently authenticated as compatible with a twelfth-century date. It is decorated with bishops and lions – perhaps representing Church and state, the joint masters of the city. *Photograph John Crook*

National administration, well established by Henry II, continued effectively during Richard's absences. During the Lionheart's reign Winchester Castle enjoyed fifth place in expenditure behind the Tower, Dover, Oxford and York. Richard died in 1199, after which the throne passed to his brother John (1199-1216), among the most mobile of English kings. In his 17½ year reign he never spent more than a month in one place. Thus it is not surprising to find Winchester one staging-post among many, and in the course of his reign it fell to eighteenth in terms of residential expenditure.

During Richard and John's reigns the city developed its privileges. Unlike episcopal towns where the domination of the bishop could be absolute, Winchester enjoyed divided lordship after Henry II took back the royal properties which were in Henry of Blois's hands in 1148. In honour of his coronation at Winchester in 1189 (no doubt with an associated financial settlement by the city), Richard confirmed the privileges of the city's gild merchant (see Glossary), and gave added permission for it to plead cases outside the walls, a freedom or urban life sought after in the Middle Ages. City walls were another proof of urban identity. Winchester had developed its own seal by *c.*1200 which shows five crenellated gate towers. As in many towns, the gild merchant became synonymous with the city government *c.*1200 and the first reference to a mayor is found around this date.

John's reign was a watershed in terms of grants of city charters. In 1215, the same year as Magna Carta, he granted a charter (no longer extant) to Winchester confirming its privileges. After Runnymede, in the civil war between king and barons, the latter supported by Louis, son of Philip II of France, Winchester Castle was captured after two weeks' siege. The attacking baronial army under Louis filled the ditch and breached the walls. However, with John's death the point of the war was lost and in 1217 the castle, after having been battered by attacks from both within and without the walls of the city, was recaptured for John's young son, Henry III.

HENRY III AND PETER DES ROCHES

Henry III (1216-72) was the most enthusiastic monarch for Winchester. He was born there in 1207, baptised in the cathedral, and during his minority came under the influence of its bishop, Peter des Roches (1205-38). This great bishop was an engineer and diplomat as well as one of the few crusaders to enter Jerusalem at the head of an army, which he did in 1229. The king's obvious love of fine architecture, which he did much to improve in the city, may have been derived from des Roches. Henry spent Christmas at Winchester 18 times in his 56 year reign.

Building work at Winchester is often loosely described as Henry III's. Early in the reign, however, Peter des Roches was the moving force. His campaign involved major works, notably the replacement after 1222 of the square keep of the castle by a functional, fashionable round one (Biddle 2000, 60). This was followed by a remodelling of the towers of the castle in the new rounded style. In the same year he began the rebuilding of the castle's great hall at a cost of £500. This magnificent building is the finest example of secular work from Henry III's reign still in existence (*41* and *colour plate 9*), although later altered in building campaigns of the fourteenth and nineteenth centuries. Henry III spent £10,000 in Winchester during his reign, when chapels as well as chambers, decorated in green and embellished with stars, were added to the castle and echoed in the cathedral (see *colour plate 8*).

Archaeological excavation and detailed study of mortars have shown that the city walls were rebuilt in the thirteenth century. This rebuilding may have accompanied the campaigns in the last years of John's reign or, alternatively, was a reaction to the failure of the walls to keep out John's opponents. If the latter, then Bishop des Roches may well have been the architect. The thirteenth-century rebuilding of the Roman wall was substantial, involving a refacing with ashlar blocks and flints. The largest section of the city walls still to be seen is found south of Wolvesey and along the Weirs, standing to a height of some 6m (20ft).

If work on the castle and city walls was a benefit of the minority period, so was the granting of a charter to the city in 1227. It echoed the Johannine charter of 1215, but with additional clauses, perhaps the most important of which was the promise that a royal mint would remain in Winchester forever. However, the young king could not sustain that promise, and 16 years later in 1243, the final coins were struck at the Winchester mint. Moneyers had long been significant members of society in Winchester, and this disappearance represents a significant diminution of royal patronage.

As one benefit ceased, another began. Two mills in the Coitebury are (around Eastgate Street), granted to the city by Henry III, were perhaps in themselves useful but not outstanding gifts. However, from these small property holdings – the first to be owned

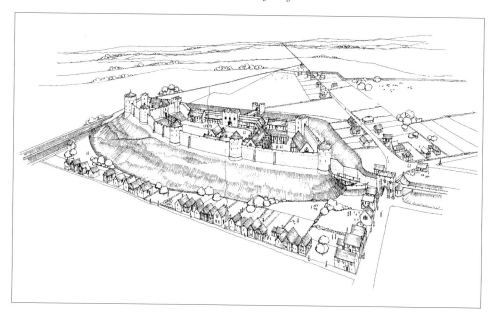

40 Reconstruction of the castle at the time of Henry III (born 1207 at Winchester, reigned 1216-72). Henry's magnificent hall, abutting the east wall, survives, and parts of the round towers, fragments of which, with their sally-ports, are displayed north of the hall. *Drawn by John Reynolds; Copyright Hampshire County Council*

41a Winchester Castle Great Hall, built under Bishop des Roches, overseen by Elias de Dereham *c*.1222-36. In 1787, seen here, the original entrance at the low end of the hall – later moved to the centre – is visible and the hall retains its later medieval appearance with afragment of the castle wall on the city side, attached. *Author's collection*

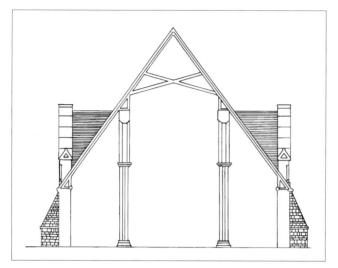

41b Winchester Castle Great Hall. The section shows how the hall might have looked in its thirteenth-century form. Traces of the upstanding '*stantivis*' window gables can be seen (in *colour plate 9*) above the fourteenth-century windows, inserted in a maintenance campaign at the time of the Black Death in 1349. *Drawn by Philip Marter*

by the city government – grew wealth which made the city authorities rivals to the king and the Church as landlords within the walls. Ultimately the proportion was to outstrip other landowners, gaining some 30 per cent of property in the city after the Reformation (see *colour plates 8* and *9*).

On his return from the Holy Land in 1231 Bishop des Roches set in place a new jurisdiction in the southern and eastern suburbs of the city, perhaps to secure income from these areas. These extramural lands were known collectively as The Soke, and were extended by Bishop William Raleigh (1240-50) to include part of the street outside West Gate and a similar area outside North Gate. These represent substantial areas and reflect not only the power and organizational ability of Bishop Peter, but also growth in population.

THE BARONS' WAR

Poor relations between Henry III (who prevented the bishop gaining access to his diocesan lands from his election in 1240 until 1244) and Bishop Raleigh were indicative of increasingly bad relations with the nobility and churchmen which culminated in the Barons' War of 1263-7. Henry III carried out considerable work on the castle: in 1243 the ditch was widened; in the 1250s work continued on the defences so that by 1258, when violence flared, all the towers in its eastern wall (against the city) had been rebuilt, rounded and high to the best contemporary specifications (see *40* and *41a*).

Raleigh's successor was the king's young half-brother Aymer of Lusignan (1250-60) otherwise known as de Valence, who contributed a Purbeck marble screen to enclose the shrine of St Swithun (*42*). However, he paid a price for being a foreigner and for his relationship to the king, as the focus of the conflict in the summer of 1258 was a siege by baronial forces of his Wolvesey Palace, and he was expelled from England.

Perhaps also in 1258-9, possibly because the economy of the city was ailing and so interruptions to trade the more unfortunate, further tensions became apparent between groups in the city. City people alleged that the prior and monks had blocked various city gates by which traders came to market. Such measures may have been part of the defensive scheme against the baronial besiegers of Wolvesey. The baronial forces enjoyed sufficient success in 1258 to force the king to agree to the Provisions of Oxford. But the tide turned in Henry III's favour and in 1261 a parliament at the castle hall at Winchester repudiated the Provisions. Some, perhaps limited, royalist support in the city, together with the strengthened defences of the castle, enabled the king on this occasion to reward the city with this symbolic ceremony.

However, the king's temporary victory did not eradicate tensions between sectors of the population of Winchester. In 1264, a week before Henry III was captured at the battle of Lewes, Winchester citizens attacked the cathedral priory burning both the King's and Prior's Gates. The king took hasty action to protect the Winchester Jews who were under attack in the confused political circumstances of the time. In a final flourish of baronial success before their cause was destroyed and Simon de Montfort killed at the battle of Evesham in August 1265, Winchester was captured by the younger Simon de Montfort, an event accompanied by further attacks on the Jews in the city. The castle held out, although there was damage to property in its vicinity during the fighting.

After 1265 Henry III enjoyed seven years of personal rule. His death in 1272 represents the end of an era in the city. He was the first post-Conquest monarch to be buried at Westminster Abbey. This was the opening move in the creation of a mausoleum in England to match that of the Capetian dynasty at St Denis, outside Paris. Winchester Castle remained a strongpoint, but building there all but ceased after 1272.

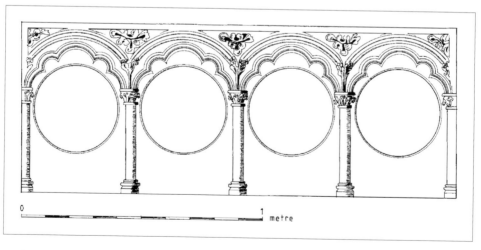

42 A reconstruction of fragments, now on display in the Triforium gallery, of a Purbeck shrine, probably Swithun's. *Drawing and Copyright John Crook*

THE JEWISH COMMUNITY

A Jewish cemetery was established on the hillside outside West Gate by 1177 and was partly excavated in the mid-1990s at Mews Lane (WMSN 22, 1995). By 1250, Jews had become a powerful force in the city. That de Montfort was against them and Henry III for them can be confidently asserted: no doubt because by borrowing from the Jews Henry side-stepped the need for grants from the pro-Montfortian parliament. With the return of Henry III's personal rule after 1265, the Jews prospered in Winchester, based around Jewry Street.

In 1268 Benedict the Jew was admitted freeman of the gild merchant, the earliest surviving record of any admission to the guild, and no doubt an event worthy of record. But de Montfort was not the only enemy of the Jews, as is evidenced by the need to issue a further edict for their protection in 1270, in which year the cathedral priory agreed to pay the large sum of £100 as damages to Winchester Jewry. Nationally the Jewish Community was already unpopular with Edward I, Henry III's son and successor, when in 1287 Assher the Jew etched his name in the wall of the castle while imprisoned there. Finally, in 1290, all Jews were expelled from England, not to be seen again in Winchester for centuries.

EDWARD I

Edward I (1272-1307) did not return from crusading until 1274. The king, well known for his Welsh castles, saw that Winchester Castle was maintained and that works were done, such as the rebuilding of the bridge over the ditch at the western entrance. Winchester's association with King Arthur may have been the reason why, in the wake of the rediscovery of 'Arthur's grave' at Glastonbury, a round table was made. The Arthurian connection cannot be proved, but the table, still to be seen hanging on the wall of the great hall, was made c.1290 (*43*) (Biddle 2000 and see below for a discussion of a possible fourteenth-century date). So far as Edward I was concerned, the myth of Arthur was propaganda against the Welsh, but became entwined with the folklore of Winchester.

Winchester served Edward I in a number of ways. It provided a solemn setting for the enactment of the Statue of Winchester (1285) which concerned the keeping of the peace. On other occasions it was a secure prison for a range of offenders, including Jews and, after 1290, Welsh and then Scots military prisoners.

Although Winchester was not a favourite haunt of Edward's first wife Eleanor of Castile, a tile representation of her coat of arms has been recovered in the city. A plausible reconstruction of an Eleanor of Castile garden has been created on the south side of the great hall of the castle in recent years. The garden has turf seats, an open water-channel with a fountain (modelled on one mentioned in the records at the king's hawkhouse at Charing Cross with additional, local, Winchester details), an arbour with a camomile lawn and a pleached alley. Plants are restricted to those known to have been in favour in the thirteenth century.

43 The Round
Table in 1873. It was
clearly once a table
as can be seen by
the broken mortices
which formerly
attached the legs.
*Copyright Hampshire
Record Office
65M89/2250 (part)*

THE FRIARS

The contrast between the wealth of kings and bishops of Winchester and the ancient
priory and the poverty of the orders of friars, which arrived in England in the 1290s, is
as sharp as any distinction to be made in the Middle Ages. The friars came to England
fired with zeal to live in poverty and help the urban poor in particular. At Winchester
the Dominicans gained an extensive site to establish a major house, inside the East Gate
to the north of the High Street: the availability of land within the walls may be an early
indication of shrinkage of population and settlement, for at Oxford and elsewhere that
had to be content with extra-mural sites. As was so common for religious communities
whose mission was to serve the poor, the Franciscans and Dominicans found themselves
the receivers of donations, and in time their friaries became popular as desirable burial
places. Their houses at Winchester, as elsewhere, became comparatively richly appointed

as the recovery of high-status glazed tiles from their East Gate and South Gate sites show.

One nuance of social and religious change which can be demonstrated by archaeology from the thirteenth century was the emergence of the practice of burial within the nuns' church at St Mary. With the arrival of the friars, whose house became a popular burial place for the wealthy, no doubt in return for generous funds for the poor. It could be argued that the nuns needed to have something special to offer their patrons: looking after the remains of patrons and ancestors by nuns at Fontevrault and elsewhere is well attested.

PEOPLE AND BUILDINGS

If the city population fell to 8000 just before 1150 it may have benefited from the marked population rise in the country at large in the century that followed. In 1300 the population may have been stagnating at 8000 but more likely had grown to about 11,625 including the suburbs (Keene 1985; James 1988).

The city was dominated by the great monuments of king and Church. The built environment of their contemporary townspeople has usually to be recovered by excavation. There are no complete standing houses of the period 1150-1300, although in Chesil Street in the Soke most of the original roof of a timber-framed house of the late thirteenth century has recently been discovered intact and has been dated by dendro-chronology to the winter of 1292-3: a unique survival of that period and the oldest town house in Hampshire (Roberts 2003).

Excavation has revealed much about living conditions among dwellers in the city in the twelfth and thirteenth centuries. Excavations at Lower Brook Street (1960s) and the Brooks (1987-8) have revealed evidence of housing of this date. At present such information as there is on these structures is available only from interim reports, supported by the finds volumes from the 1960s' excavations.

A two-storeyed, flint rubble house set back from the street, for example, was already in place in Lower Brook Street by 1150. Its narrow, splayed windows, of a kind often found in churches, are typical of the period. The space between this house and the street was occupied by flimsy wooden structures, no doubt shops and/or workshops. It is clear that there was a mixture of high-status stone and timber-framed houses built together in this area of the city. One timber building, known as Lower Brook Street, House 1, was a simple, single-storeyed timber structure which developed into a complex stone structure of two storeys combining domestic and industrial premises by 1200 (see 47).

Just to the north, the Brooks excavations revealed a similar pattern of both stone and timber houses and workshops. On the Upper Brook Street (de Tytynge) site, the single wooden tenement of tenth- or eleventh-century date was divided into three tenements in the twelfth century, the buildings being reconstructed in stone. On the Middle Brook Street side of the site a fuller's property of twelfth-century date (44) apparently stood on the street frontage with wooden structures and workshops behind. In both cases the street frontages had been covered by subsequent street widening (itself an indication of

44 Upper Brook Street, looking east. The central property, with gates to the street and a hall and other buildings behind, had a complex development from before the Norman Conquest, perhaps being at its most substantial *c.*1300 when it belonged to John de Tytynge, alderman of the street. After the Black Death it was inhabited by poor people and was demolished *c.*1377. The fuller's property (top left) faced Middle Brook Street. *After Graham Scobie; drawn by Philip Marter*

the dereliction of this area in the post-medieval period), which left the archaeologists struggling to re-create the fronts of the houses, although arrangements towards the rear of the sites were more easy to recover and interpret (*44*).

What is plain from the present evidence is that in the Brooks area there was mixed housing in the twelfth and thirteenth centuries, and industrial zoning, with ample evidence of activities involved with textile industry to the fore. Analysis from the

1960s' excavations shows a clear rise in quantity of finds of thirteenth-century date, which is consistent with high population and the prosperity characterised by the major monuments.

CHURCHES

The twelfth and thirteenth centuries saw a peak in the number of churches in Winchester, both within and outside the walls. The total, about 1300, was made up of the cathedral priory, two abbeys, four friaries, four non-parochial chapels (not including various private chapels, for example at the castle) and 54 parish churches. The distribution of the parish churches which have been located can be seen on the 1148 map (see *36*), with a concentration around the wealthy High Street. Of this great body of churches only seven are now standing, and these have limited twelfth-and thirteenth-century work. Excavation has taken place on seven demolished churches, mostly notably St Mary, Tanner Street, and St Pancras, both adjacent in the Brooks area. These show development and expansion in the twelfth and thirteenth centuries. At St Peter in Macellis, St George Street, there were enlargements which included the addition of an apse of some 3m (10ft) diameter, and a north aisle probably built in the twelfth or thirteenth century. In similar fashion at St Anastasius, the siting of the north wall further north in the late thirteenth century suggests the incorporation of an aisle. At the surviving St John in The Soke a fine series of thirteenth-century wall paintings was still to be seen in the nineteenth century, when they were largely destroyed, although subsequent clearance of blocked thirteenth-century windows revealed surviving fragments of that scheme in the splays, where the representations of St John the Evangelist and St Christopher are found. As a whole the evidence from the parish churches is consistent with recorded growth of the city and with well-attested trends in church architecture in the two centuries before 1300.

6

WAR AND PLAGUE
1300-1485

THE BUILT ENVIRONMENT

The city was as populous in 1300 as at anytime in the Middle Ages, but the following two centuries saw significant decline. Developments in the built environment are more readily comprehensible to the modern eye, for many types of structures created at this time still remain. This is the first period for which domestic and commercial properties survive in the city both within the walls and in the suburbs.

The cathedral took the form in which we see it today, with the demolition of the Norman west towers and their replacement after 1350 with the great west window in the Perpendicular style. In The Close, the remains of the monastic buildings which survive today include notable timber-framed structures of the fourteenth and fifteenth centuries, including the Pilgrims' Hall (1310-11), the Deanery (formerly the Prior's Lodgings, 1459), and the stables. The church of St Cross was completed after 1350, and its residential accommodation replaced by 1450. Winchester College appeared in the southern suburb by 1400, an indication of the availability of land after the Black Death. The West Gate as we see it today is largely late fourteenth century in date (see *31*).

Many buildings, not in existence in 1150, would have been visible to visitors in the fourteenth and fifteenth centuries, but have since disappeared. The friaries, especially the Dominican and Franciscan houses inside East Gate, were notable additions in the thirteenth century. Recent excavations of the house of Austin Friars outside the site of the former South Gate showed a spacious building of stone, with coloured tiles on the floor and fragments of tombs hinting at the patronage which made such grand buildings possible (Simon Roffey, pers. comm.). This work demonstrates how the friars' urban mission was rewarded with rich donations in the later Middle Ages. It also reminds us that the high population of the city at this time bred much poverty, which it was the friars' mission to alleviate.

Royal influence wanes in this period, and ecclesiastical developments – for example at the cathedral priory, St Cross, Winchester College and Wolvesey – mask a general decline in the city's economy, which led to some 'fossilisation' accounting for the comparatively numerous late medieval standing remains in the city today. Parish churches, however, declined in numbers and many disappeared.

The principal features of the fourteenth- and fifteenth-century layout were: the streets, the scale of domestic and shop accommodation in relation to the great buildings of cathedral and bishop's palace, and market places such as that marked by the Buttercross in High Street. Many areas of the city, especially north of High Street and in the suburbs, became gardens, particularly in the fifteenth century. Around High Street and elsewhere, the form of plots preserves the dimensions of late medieval gardens, and property leases make reference to such appurtenances.

THE END OF ROYAL RESIDENCE

When fire broke out in the royal apartments of the castle in 1302, Edward I and Queen Margaret were asleep but managed to escape. Full repairs were probably never carried out at the castle. This marks a key stage in the reduction of Winchester's royal role. However, occasional high-status finds from the castle – such as a green glass goblet, indicative of wine-drinking, from the period c.1300 – illuminate the quality of life in that late stage of royal use.

From early in the fourteenth century the royal entourage usually stayed at Wolvesey. There was considerable political uncertainty in the 1320s and 1330s: civil war, followed by war with France. The city probably favoured Edward II (1307-27) in the struggle against his queen, Isabella. Winchester was established as a wool staple town in 1326 and retained that status until 1353. The loss of the civil war by Edward II led to retribution. Thus the earl of Winchester was beheaded by Isabella's supporters in 1327 at Bristol and his head transported to Winchester castle to be displayed above its gate.

WAR AGAINST FRANCE

The end of the Capetian dynasty in 1328 made possible an English claim to the throne of France. This claim led to war with France: the Hundred Years' War broke out in 1337. A destructive raid on Southampton in October 1338 caused alarm in Hampshire and works on Winchester's walls were carried out in 1338-9.

The early years of the war were extravagantly financed so that by 1340 the treasury was empty and there was a crisis. The remarkable wool weights, 91lb (quarter sack), 56lb (half hundredweight) and 28lb (tod) which survive in Winchester from the 1350s, were associated with the city's status as a staple town and perhaps with the move of the weigh-beam (trona) to a new site in 1353 (Stevenson, n.d.), may have been part of a drive for greater revenue. They echo the war in that they bear a royal coat of arms quartered with those of France, which Edward III had assumed with the title 'king of France' in 1340.

45 The west end of the Cathedral showing the break in stone-building styles which occurred around the time of the Black Death in the mid-fourteenth century. The triple porch below in the labour-intensive, expensive, French, Decorated style, and the great west window in the cheap, mass-produced, Perpendicular, English style of the post-plague era, above. *Photo and copyright John Crook*

War dragged on until 1453 and affected the city intermittently. For example, after 1369 when the French threatened the south coast, royal orders were issued for the repair of the walls and these orders perhaps led to the repointing of the walls of Winchester with yellow mortar and flints which have been founded embedded in the north, west and east walls of the city. The machicolations and grand refurbishment of the West Gate are also suggestive of a late fourteenth-century date (see *31*). Durn Gate, located at the north eastern extremity of the walls, was rapidly walled up at this time at the insistence of a local alderman.

By *c.*1400 the castle was not always fit for royal visitors. Visits by Richard II and Anne of Bohemia (1393), and by Henry V in 1415, involved ecclesiastical accommodation: in Richard's reign Bishop Wykeham was the host; in Henry V's reign it was Cardinal Beaufort, the king's cousin. However, when Henry IV and Joan of Navarre came to Winchester in 1402 for their marriage they stayed at the castle, perhaps because Bishop Wykeham was too elderly to receive them.

In the 1420s during the minority of Henry VI, the history of the ancient capital was being carefully managed. At about 1425 a mortuary chest, said to contain the remains of kings Egbert and Kenulph, was replaced with a fine painted chest, now to be seen on display at the Triforium gallery. Not only was the Lancastrian dynasty vulnerable during a minority – Henry VI had inherited in 1422 as a baby of nine months – and so needed bolstering in all possible ways, but also Cardinal Beaufort was illegitimate. His grand coat of arms with the motif of his cardinal's hat, still to be seen displayed in the glass of the hall windows at St Cross, was intended to give substance to a member of a family barred by statute from the throne.

PLAGUE AND POPULATION

With the loss of royal status and a levelling of population from the late thirteenth century, growth in the city slackened. The Black Death of 1348-50 ushered in three centuries in which demographic development was dominated by plague. The disease and its economic effects added to the difficulties Winchester was encountering with the loss of royal status. There is some doubt about when and where the plague broke out. The chronicler Knighton claimed Southampton as the port of entry, and it may have been, in the summer of 1348. In November 1348 Bishop Edington of Winchester issued mandates for prayers for penance 'on account of unexpected death' to be offered to the Winchester monasteries and Nunnaminster because of plague (Hockey 1987, ii, 25). By Christmas 1348 the disease had taken an even stronger grip, and significant mortality was occurring across Hampshire and elsewhere in his diocese (Watts 1998; Arthur 2005). Urban populations were especially at risk from the plague and Winchester was no exception with its dense housing, malnutrition and poor sanitation.

Anaerobic deposits in the Brooks excavations in the 1960s contained evidence of parasites and plague bacilli. The effects of the plague on the clergy of the city and diocese can be charted in bishop Edington's register (Hockey 1986, 1987, *passim*). Winchester diocese was hit hardest in England with an estimated 48 per cent mortality among clergy. The cathedral priory was hard pressed and numbers fell from around 60 before the plague to some 35 thereafter until the Dissolution. At the 'Sustren Spital', a hospital community of women in the southern suburb, there were normally 21 inmates, but after the plague this fell to 6, increasing to 10 in 1352-3, but never to more than 16 thereafter. Men were admitted in the later Middle Ages. The effects on the lay population of the city are more difficult to monitor, but we do know that a dispute was carried to the royal government about graveyard space around the cathedral where the high death toll

Above: 1 Aerial view of Winchester from the south showing St Catharine's Hill (right), and the historic city, before the M3 extension. Erdberi lies to the left of the cathedral (left). *Copyright Winchester Research Unit*

Right: 2 Roman Winchester *c.*AD 300 was spacious. Coloured buildings are reconstructed at The Brooks (foreground) and Woolworth's site, High Street (centre). The Forum buildings (top) ran west and south of the site where The Pentice stands today, covering the whole width of the Roman High Street. *After Winchester City Archaeology Office; drawn by Dr Philip Marter*

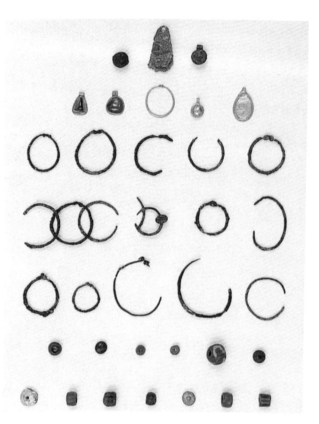

Left and below: 3 A Saxon necklace of gold, silver, garnets and beads found on the skeleton of an aristocratic and perhaps royal young woman in grave 23, Lower Brook Street, dated to *c.*650-700. The letters on the plan correspond to the catalogue entries in Winchester Studies 7(ii): A-Z (1957-1982), AA-AV (1983-2004). Row 1 (1961, 1957, 1962); Row 2 (1958-9, 1989, 1963, 1960); Row 3 1965-72; Row 4 (1974-5, 1991 with 1978, 1980-2); Row 5 1983, 1985-7, 1990); Row 6 (1992-7); Row 7 (1998-2004). *Copyright Winchester Research Unit*

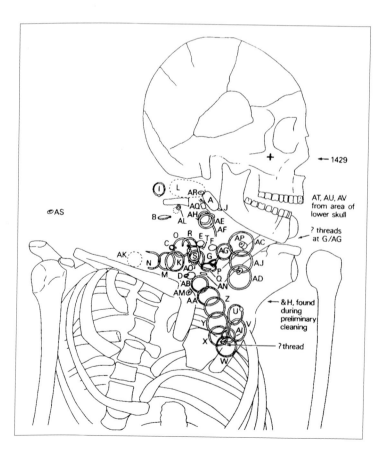

Above: 4 The Norman crypt of the cathedral: east end of the central chamber looking north. The crypt is the earliest work in the cathedral and preserves the plan of the Norman apse, now lost above-ground. The well lies at the approximate geometrical centre of the apse and the original high altar was placed, purposefully, directly above it. *Photograph and copyright John Crook*

Right: 5 The apse of Hyde Abbey, north of the city, which was occupied by Benedictine monks from New Minster in 1110. Hyde incorporated one of the largest monastic churches in medieval England. This picture shows the arrangement of the east end of the church, revealed by a community archaeology project, with three markers indicating the graves of King Alfred and others before the site of the former high altar with the steel-enclosed trees marking the sites of former columns. The inset shows a reconstruction of Hyde Abbey by Tracey Sheppard. Celebrations of the foundation of Hyde Abbey are scheduled for 2010. *Photograph and copyright Barbara Hall*

Top: 6 Reconstruction of the Old Bishop's Palace at Wolvesey, looking north-east. The bishop's chapel in the foreground, rebuilt in the later Middle Ages, is still in use. *Drawn by Terry Ball; copyright English Heritage, 1986*

Above: 7 An illuminated capital from the Winchester Bible, associated with Henry of Blois, *c.*1160. A bishop, perhaps Henry himself, holds a book. *Copyright Dean and Chapter*

8 Guardian Angels' Chapel in the Cathedral of *c.*1240. This is a rare survival in an ecclesiastical context of the rich decoration familiar in palaces and great churches in the reign of Henry III (1216–72). The exceptional range of colours and pigments, including blue surrounding the gilded stars is likely to be derived from crushed lapis lazuli, brought then from Afghanistan. This was the most extravagant of all materials, including gold. *Photograph and copyright John Crook*

9 The Great Hall, Winchester castle, built for Henry III under the watchful eye of Elias de Dereham c.1230. After Westminster Hall, this is the greatest surviving royal hall of medieval England. Both the scale of the hall and the structural use of Purbeck for the columns mark this out as an important and exceptional building.
Photograph and copyright John Crook

10 St John, the prophet Zephaniah and St James, part of Thomas of Oxford's glazing scheme of the 1390s for Winchester College chapel. These panels are now in the Victoria and Albert Museum. *Copyright RCHME*

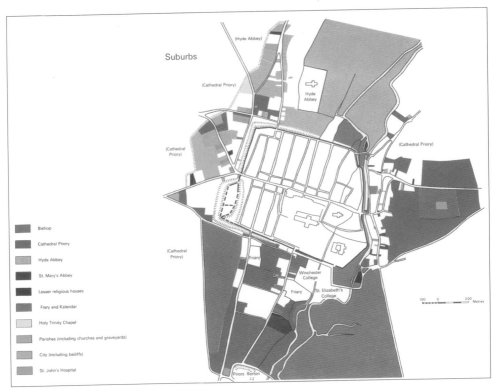

Suburbs

Bishop
Cathedral Priory
Hyde Abbey
St. Mary's Abbey
Lesser religious houses
Frary and Kalendar
Holy Trinity Chapel
Parishes (including churches and graveyards)
City (including bailiffs)
St. John's Hospital

(Hyde Abbey)
(Cathedral Priory)
Hyde Abbey
(Cathedral Priory)
(Cathedral Priory)
(Cathedral Priory)
Friary
Winchester College
Friary
St. Elizabeth's College
Priors Barton

100   0   200
Metres

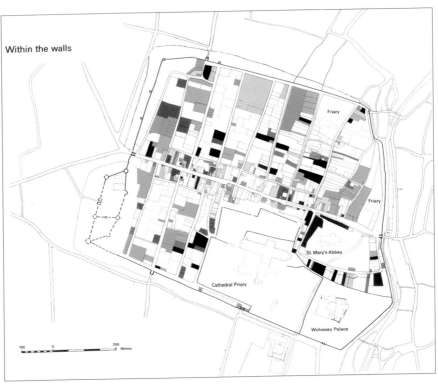

Within the walls

Friary
Friary
St. Mary's Abbey
Cathedral Priory
Wolvesey Palace

100   0   200
Metres

11 1417. Plans of institutions' landholdings. The Church dominates the suburbs; within the walls St John's Hospital and the city are dominant. *Winchester Research Unit*

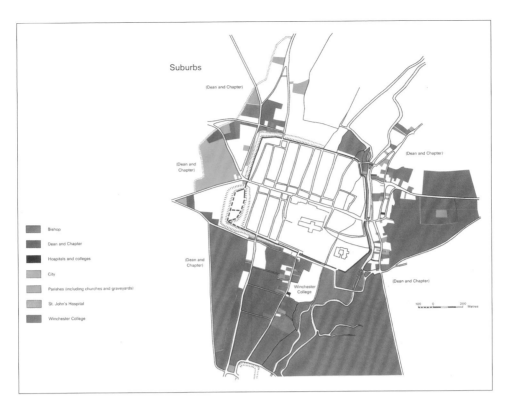

Suburbs

(Dean and Chapter)

(Dean and Chapter)

(Dean and Chapter)

(Dean and Chapter)

(Dean and Chapter)

(Dean and Chapter)

Winchester College

Bishop

Dean and Chapter

Hospitals and colleges

City

Parishes (including churches and graveyards)

St. John's Hospital

Winchester College

100   0   200 Metres

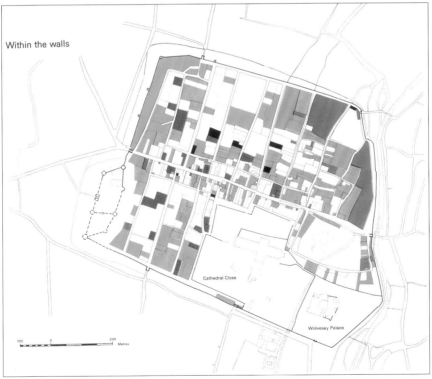

Within the walls

Cathedral Close

Wolvesey Palace

100   0   200 Metres

12 1590. Plans of institutions' landholdings. The lands of the bishop and of the Dean and Chapter (successors of the cathedral priory) survive unimpaired. Within the walls, the city government have benefited since the Reformation, and Winchester College's main prizes are two large former Friary sites. *Winchester Research Unit*

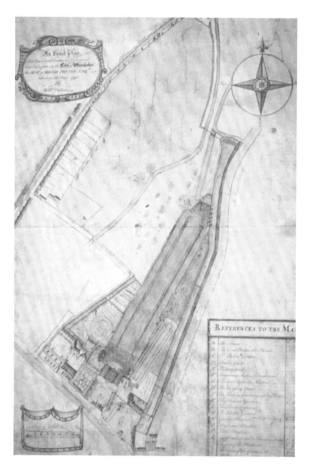

13 1748. St John's House (left) and chapel. Henry Penton's mansion and garden (centre) are near East Gate on the former Blackfriars site, which had passed to Winchester College at the Dissolution. *Copyright Hampshire Record Office, 147M86W/1*

14 1801. Cathedral Choir. The altar soundboard (1635) and organ-case figures (c.1665) are preserved in the Triforium Gallery; the screen urns are lost. *Photograph John Crook; copyright Dean and Chapter*

15 Reconstruction of the cathedral shrine of Swithun, erected *c.*1478 and demolished *c.*1538. *By Judith Dobie and reproduced by permission of the Dean and Chapter*

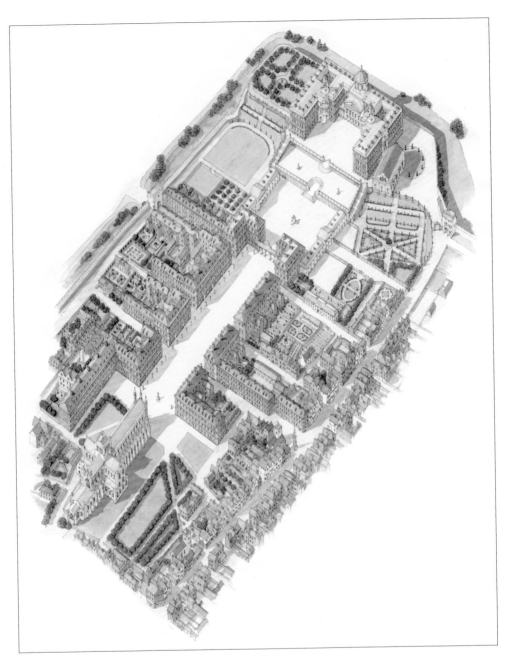

Above: 16 Winchester as it might have been as envisaged by Charles II in his plan to incorporate Cathedral and a new palace into a royal complex to match Versailles. The vision was never realised, but the details of how such a scheme might have appeared are shown here. *Drawing and copyright Stephen Conlin*

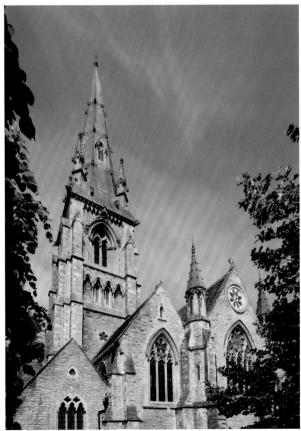

Above: 17 The Corn Exchange in Jewry Street designed by Owen Browne Carter in the 1830s, prior to the arrival of the railway, originally planned to terminate nearby. The Italianate style and London brick echo Prince Albert's creation at Osborne on the Isle of Wight. *Photograph Frank Chippindale; author's collection*

Right: 18 New St Thomas's Church. Southgate Street of *c.*1850 in the Decorated style, acknowledged as the grandest of the Gothic Revival churches in Winchester. Part of the price paid was the demolition of the historic namesake church in St Thomas's Street. *Photograph John Crook*

19 Diocesan Training College by John Colson, 1862. The Gothic Revival building with its polychrome roof reminds the viewer of Winchester's late medieval educational heritage. There are some additional features drawn from contemporary French Second Empire style, for example in the tower. The training college was part of an early 'welfare state' development on the West Hill, designed to manage the masses from cradle to grave: old and young, healthy and sick, criminal, worker and unemployed, and included cemetery, hospital, police headquarters, prison, national school, training college and workhouse. *Author's collection*

Opposite above: 20 West Downs building, University of Winchester. This former national school and subsequently preparatory school was purchased by the University of Winchester in recent years as a site of a second campus on the West Hill. Together with its Arts and Crafts Masters' Lodge of 1905 it has been renovated and the campus now houses teaching spaces, a student village and the University's Research and Knowledge Transfer Centre. *Photograph and copyright University of Winchester*

Opposite below: 21 1993. Twyford Down during the removal of over 2 million cubic metres of chalk for motorway construction. As 'extreme and irreversible an act of environmental spoiling as can be imagined' thundered *The Times* leader. *Copyright Twyford Down Association*

22 The University's former Dining Hall and kitchens, photographed in 1969 within ten years of being built in 1962 to designs by Woodroffe, Buchanan and Coulter. This 'collapsed-tent roof' style as Nikolaus Pevsner described it, with its large windows and buttresses constituted a 'true' Gothic building, creating architectural resonances with the Gothic Revival, adjacent Main Building of 1862 and is in turn commemorated in the University Centre. *Photograph Frank Chippindale; Author's collection*

23 The University Centre, currently under construction on Sparkford Road for the University from the south-west. The architects have drawn on elements of the previous structure on the site, the now-demolished Dining Hall and kitchens. The scale of this structure reflects the rise in numbers in higher education in Winchester from the few dozen of 1862 to some 6000 today. *Copyright University of Winchester*

filled up the available plots and led to encroachment on adjacent property as seen in figure *28*. In January 1349 a monk, recognisable by his tonsure and dress, was attacked while conducting a burial in the priory (cathedral) burial ground. In February 1352 a royal grant was made because of the 'waste and depression on the city from the time when the deadly pestilence last prevailed', a view supported by archaeological evidence that during and immediately after the Black Death organised rubbish disposal in the city may have broken down. Winchester was among places devastated by the Black Death. Plague returned fiercely in 1361 and regularly thereafter until the seventeenth century (for the Black Death in Winchester in more detail see Keene, 1985; James 1998; WMSN 27, 1997).

POPULATION AND CEMETERIES

The tarrage roll for 1417 lists 839 tenements, excluding The Soke, which perhaps contained 40 per cent of the population. The information can be translated into 6921 lay people and an estimated 789 clergy – total 7710. These figures represent a decline from the higher estimated population in 1300, but are on a par with the lower estimate (James 1988). By 1450 the population had more certainly declined when petitions from the city to central government referred to 987 empty houses in the city. The population probably decreased towards the end of the fifteenth century.

It is possible from their excavated bones to make some comments about the physical and medical characteristics of the inhabitants of the city in the three centuries preceding 1450. Many bones were uncovered in the 1960s and preliminary results show that arthritis afflicted the majority of Winchester skeletons analysed; there were a number of bone tumours – some perhaps tubercular, others carcinogenic. In a small number of instances syphilis or an allied disease may be indicated by a roughening of the bone surface, particularly on the long bones. It is noteworthy that plague, among other diseases, leaves no mark upon bones.

Thirty-six graves, presumably from patrons and their families and of nuns, have been excavated from the ruins of St Mary's Abbey. These human remains date from the mid-thirteenth century down to the Dissolution. An equal number of men and women were buried in the nunnery. Seven females lived to over 45: none of the men did. Whether or not women came from the abbey is unknown, but dietary deficiency together with arthritis and other diseases can be shown to have affected people even at this exalted level of society (www.cityofwinchester.co.uk/history/history.html and Winchester Museums Service for details of the Nunnaminster).

THE GREAT REVOLT

The Great or Peasants' Revolt of 1381 over the poll tax provided an opportunity for a general settling of disputes. Potential existed for friction between ecclesiastical and lay society in Winchester and, echoing the thirteenth century, this may have been one of the motives for violence in the city in 1381. However, it may have been that the immense wealth of the see and the priory took some of the force out of such feelings, for the institutions offered sustained economic activity in the great building campaigns of the later fourteenth and fifteenth centuries.

Anger, sparked by tensions among the citizens, was directed primarily against the royal government. Fourteen out of twenty-five of those recorded in Hampshire, who were executed or who fled after the Great Revolt, came from Winchester. The focus of the Revolt was the lower High Street in the cloth-finishing area of the city: Tanner Street, Colebrook Street and the area around the church of St George. William Wygge, perhaps the ringleader, was involved with others at Winchester and elsewhere. He was a member of the guild with responsibilities in local government: the Revolt was by no means only a peasant affair. Wygge obtained a pardon and went on to be five times mayor of the city (Keene 1985, 396).

HOUSING AND INDUSTRY

The period after the plague of 1348 was difficult for the city. The housing stock varies and there is archaeological and documentary evidence that properties went out of use. However, fine housing of late fourteenth-century date survives in the city, for example The Blue Boar (46) in the eastern suburb. However, the wealth and the status of some who took part in the Great Revolt, and the survival of a contemporary house, do not indicate that everyone in Winchester was prosperous at this time. Four single-cell cottages each c.1.6sq m (17sq ft) in area, perhaps the flimsiest houses from the fourteenth century excavated in England, were laid bare in the 1960s adjacent to St Pancras Lane (Lower Brook Street) (47). These houses and those adjacent were very dark. The medieval houses excavated at Lower Brook Street produced no fewer that 105 of 126 lamps excavated in the city in the 1960s. Two houses alone produced over 60 lamps between them, fuelling the interpretation that the activity carried on in these premises required long hours of indoor work. At higher-status properties where there were more windows, more costly wax candles were used: this produced proportionately more candle holders among the finds, for example at Wolvesey Palace, and fewer lamps in the archaeological record (Biddle 1990).

Excavation of a tenement, gable end to the street and facing on to Middle Brook Street, revealed it to be of artisan status and more substantial than the properties on Lower Brook Street. It was extended in the late fourteenth century by the addition of a workshop and fuller's tank (identified by traces of ammonia and fuller's earth) which drained into the Middle Brook.

By 1400 clothworking in England was in a state of flux. The withdrawal of the cloth industry from the city to the countryside, and the resultant impoversishment of and depopulation of the city, was prominent among the reasons given by the Winchester city government in a petition to the royal government for reduction of taxes made in 1440 and sent a second time in 1452.

46 The Blue Boar, 24 and 25 St John Street, following extensive renovation in the 1960s. The curved timbers of the front elevation are a key element in dating the structure to the fourteenth century. *Copyright RCHME*

47 This neighbourhood, north of High Street, and towards the lower, wetter (high water-levels inhibited excavation), eastern, end of the city is shown in its fourteenth-century phase with the churches of St Pancras and St Mary, Tanner Street. The fourteenth-century cottages south of St Pancras Lane were flimsy and suggest that at this time the area was a poor one. The easternmost of these properties was served by a water course at this time, and a hearth in its neighbour to the west hinted at dyeing. The southerly house on this plan, standing back from the street, was a substantial stone structure built before 1150, suggesting a wealthier period at that time. It was extended to the street frontage as space was at a premium *c.*1200. This map is a microcosm of what is known from documentary sources and of the results of excavation. *After Winchester Research Unit; redrawn by Alejandra Gutiérrez*

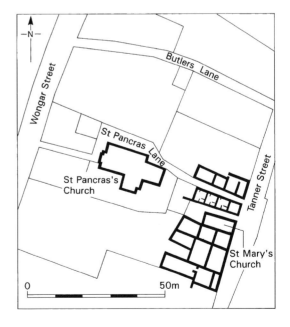

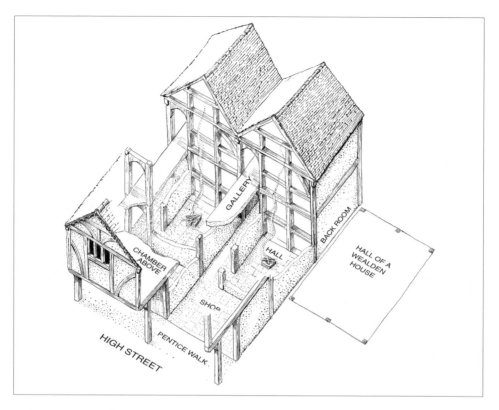

48 Reconstruction of *33* and *34* and plan of part of *35* High Street. These shops, dated by dendrochronology to 1459-62, were built at right angles to the street. They comprised purpose-built shops beside The Pentice walk, with living accommodation above and behind the shops. The spacious central hall, dendro-dated to 1340, stands parallel to the street and is all that survives of a Wealden house (part of Boots at 35 High Street, see *50* and *51*), and was one of several exceptionally large houses built in Winchester before the Black Death. It predates any such structures known from the Weald, emphasising its national importance. It may originally have had lean-to shops fronting the street. The Pentice, in part at least, assumed its present appearance in 1459-62. In 1340 it clearly looked very different. *Drawn by Judith Dobie*

Evidence can readily be adduced to show how the city changed both demographically and economically after the Black Death. From the time of the 1361 plague onwards, the land of Godbegot, for example, was parcelled up and the principal 'manor' was broken up and let out. Elsewhere the great tenement of John de Tytynge on Upper Brook Street (see *44*) appears to have suffered a similar fate, being broken up and used by lesser folk.

Interpretation of such evidence is, however, uncertain at present, raising as well as answering questions: were the wealthy moving elsewhere in the city, and if so, where? Was it to The Soke, east of the city where houses such as The Blue Boar and the Old Chesil Rectory (which was not built as a rectory) are found? In the High Street, 33 and 34 (in The Pentice) and the Godbegot are all post-plague and before 1500 (*48*, *50* and *51*). Documentary evidence of the subdivision of tenements suggests crowding together of poorer people, but overall the evidence indicates a general fall in population of the city.

49 The Star Inn, photographed c.1885 and demolished by 1929, was a medieval, jettied building. The front was bricked over, probably in the eighteenth century. *Copyright Winchester City Museums PWCM 3535*

It is unsafe to argue, on the basis of surviving vernacular houses and shops alone: their survival represents no more than a fossilisation of Winchester after this period. Prints and photographs of nineteenth-century Winchester show many timber-framed buildings now demolished, for example on the corner of St Thomas Street and High Street, and also on the corner of Staple Gardens and High Street (49), and in Middle Brook Street. Taken together – archaeology, standing remains and documentary evidence including photographs and Speed's map of c.1611 – it can be suggested that apart from the ecclesiastical southern half of the city, there was a zoning of new buildings in the High Street, Middle Brook Street and the eastern suburb in the period 1350-1500. However, numbers of timber-framed buildings did not survive the fifteenth century, for archaeology has shown elsewhere on the Brooks that houses were demolished at that time and were replaced by gardens. For the fullers who remained, these open spaces provided area for them to dry their cloth as the excavated remains of drying-frames and equipment, including tenterhooks, has shown (Biddle 1990).

There were fortunes to be made, as the speculative developments and mercantile success of Mark le Fayre, mayor, merchant and property-developer in the early fifteenth-century shows. Le Fayre, among other activities, developed a novel building type, an

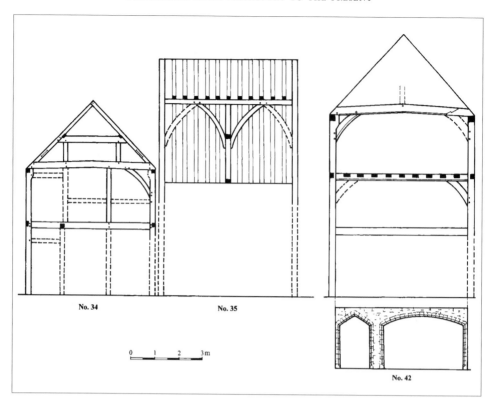

No. 34   No. 35

0   1   2   3m

No. 42

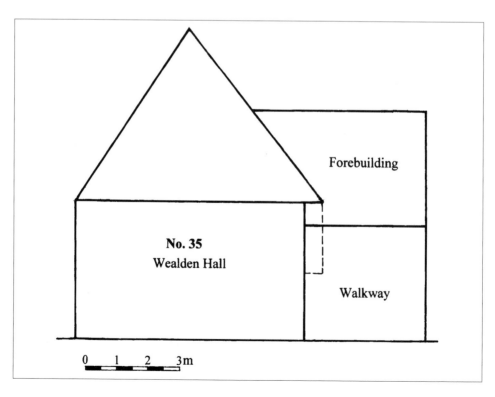

Forebuilding

No. 35
Wealden Hall

Walkway

0   1   2   3m

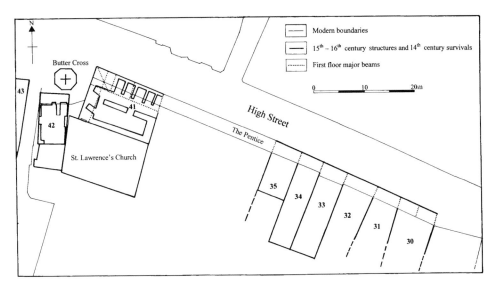

Above: 51 A plan showing the locations of two very large timber framed properties on the south side of High Street. At 35 (Boots the Chemist) the remnants of the hall of a 'Wealden'-type house, and at 42 a penticed-house of the same period, both built in the years prior to the Black Death of 1348. *Drawn by Philip Marter; reproduced by permission of the Society for Medieval Archaeology*

Opposite, above and below: 50 Figure 45 shows the changing style in stone architecture at the cathedral either side of the Black Death of 1348-50. Sections through the 'Wealden' and the great multi-storey property, with its stone basement tavern, at 42 show the great scale of these pre-plague properties. Dendrochronology shows these great structures were built before the Black Death, probably both in the 1340s. The puny scale of the shop at 34, dated to 1459-62, exemplifies how in timber building, as in stone, there was a break in building tradition, scale and style maybe attributable to the Black Death and recurrent plagues. *Drawn by Philip Marter; reproduced by permission of the Society for Medieval Archaeology*

inn, at The George before 1420. Thereafter inns became more common. The George, probably originally a large courtyard tenement with gates both to north and south, survived for a long period on the north side of the High Street and stood, although much altered, for 500 years until its demolition in 1956.

Features of the city today such at the 13m (43ft) high Buttercross (52), which signalled its eponymous market on High Street, date from the same period: Cardinal Beaufort's time as bishop, 1404-47. At St Cross fifteenth-century domestic accommodation created for the Cardinal's retainers is to be seen, massively built as individual houses to the highest specifications with parlours and latrines, enhanced by a communal hall and defended by a mighty gate tower which still bears a statue of the generous cardinal. City markets were serving a new clientele which included Wykeham's collegers.

Le Fayre was a private landlord; the city government extended its landholdings at the same period as an increasingly powerful institutional landlord of Winchester houses and other property. In the exceptional year of 1446-7, rent accounted for 88 per cent of the corporation's income. The city proved as adaptable as ever to changing circumstances.

52 The Market, or Butter Cross, was built in Cardinal Beaufort's time (died 1447). Behind the cross, with a gable, and adjacent to the west end of The Pentice lies 42 High Street, an exceptionally large medieval property of four storeys over a stone cellar. It has been dated by dendrochronology and documents to 1347. Then as now it had a penticed front, wooden pillars supporting substantial jetties. Just at the right we see the jetties of 43 High Street known in 1507 as 'le Newhouse': dendrochronology confirmed that its frame is composed of timbers cut down in that very year. We see the city's medieval fabric and pump, and also the improved paving brought about by the eighteenth-century commissioners. Wooldridge, whose shop is seen at the corner of The Pentice, was a female butcher. This view, published in 1829 was dedicated to Alexander Baring MP, of The Grange, Northington. *Drawn by Bartlett; author's collection*

LIVING STANDARDS

Central government became increasingly concerned in the fourteenth and fifteenth centuries with improving living standards, especially after the Black Death. The Statute of Labourers (1351) was an attempt to force wages back down to pre-plague levels. The

Sumptuary Law of 1363 and its successors sought to dictate what people at different levels of society should wear and eat. Anxiety about improved living standards for the lower ranks of society was clearly at fever pitch. The Winchester evidence is anecdotal, but so far as diet was concerned endorses some of the anxieties of the ruling classes.

Winchester evidence for diet in the later Middle Ages hinges on the contents of latrines. The last fill of the latrine of a large house on Upper Brook Street (see *44*) produced a wide variety of evidence of fourteenth-century diet including strawberry, fig, mulberry, cherry and plum, onion and leek, as well as a range of herbs and spices – caraway, coriander, dill and parsley. Wholemeal bread consumption is evidenced by wheat and rye bran. Human worms and fleas also found their way into the pit.

The evidence is surprisingly diverse, but in the absence of precise dating material not easy to interpret. If the contents of the latrine were contemporary with the wealthy merchant John de Tytynge's occupation of the site early in the fourteenth century, the materials may suggest some polarisation of the living standards of the population. If they come from later in the century when the structure was abandoned and the site divided, then maybe the last inhabitants of the undivided property took advantage of a buyer's market to remove themselves and to leave the low-lying site to its fate. It seems unlikely that these remains were the diet of the folk who occupied the declining property. It may simply be that new latrines were dug and an old one abandoned, or that poorer people may have relied more on public conveniences than sustaining their own provision. It may have been that certain secular inhabitants of the city continued to enjoy comfort and plenty perhaps despite declining opportunities for the population as a whole.

One effect of population stagnation and decline was that there was more wealth for those who survived the vicissitudes of the fourteenth century. So religious institutions which had previously found recruitment comparatively easy because of the high population and energetic and respected papacy, had to make themselves more appealing in a changing world. Thus, evidence from St Mary's Abbey can be seen broadly to match that from the de Tytynge site. Dietary requirements relaxed: in particular meat eating became more common on special occasions and at feasts. Meat bones in late medieval deposits in the nunnery included sheep and pig. A range of both salt-water creatures – sturgeon and dolphin – and freshwater fish from fishponds, was also found. Although this may have been the fare of abbey guests, the evidence seems clear that some survivors of the famines and plagues of the fourteenth century were able to sustain a good quality of life.

EDINGTON TO WYKEHAM

Bishop Edington had already begun to remodel the cathedral before 1350 when he demolished the westworks, which were not replaced. Edington introduced a new feature to the cathedral, indeed a new feature of ecclesiastical architecture in England, with the erection of his self-contained 'chantry' before he died in 1365. Edington's successor was William of Wykeham, a clerk in Edington's household before he was taken into royal service *c.*1350 as Edward III's clerk of works at Windsor Castle. Wykeham not only gained the diocese but also, like Edington, became Chancellor of England. Wykeham's career draws diverse elements of Winchester's development together in the most positive of ways. So far as the defences were concerned, he had the wall surrounding Wolvesey rebuilt at his own expense which drew on his experience of defensive works at Windsor.

Wykeham's second contribution to the city was Winchester College (53). This was conceived in the 1380s and work was under way by the end of the decade. One intention, as the founder's statutes show, was to produce properly educated clergy to replace those lost in the plague. The college reflects the changing face of the city. It occupies land previously inhabited, but available in the southern suburb after the Black Death. The land was downstream of the city so that the Brooks which flowed southwards carried rubbish and disease from the city: in 1398, soon after the College was opened, these watercourses were said to be full of animal remains from butchery, excreta and domestic rubbish, and a grill was inserted to prevent larger detritus from the city polluting the College water – in an age before germ-theory. In addition, French threats no doubt drove suburban dwellers into town. The severe, fortified gatehouses of the college bear testimony to the uncertain times in which they were built. The muniment tower is no less strong, and was originally reached only through iron-bound internal doors, one of which was beside the chapel altar. These were secured by large keys, while the documentary evidence of the college's endowments is kept in multi-locked trunks. Wykeham left no doubt as to the supreme importance of the endowments he provided for his college's future. His successors in the fifteenth century continued to build up the landed portfolio, for example with the rectory or priory of Andover, a market town north-west of Winchester, in 1414 where the college soon invested in the creation of the fine Angel Inn (Hare 2005; Roberts 2003).

Winchester college buildings are exceptionally fine work of their period and should be visited, especially Wykeham's hall-over-schoolroom and the chapel, built end-on in series with the hall – a match for his similar creations at New College, Oxford and at Windsor. Apart from the unique and innovative creation of a school at Winchester and a college at Oxford, each for 70 scholars, it was the sheer scale of the foundations which sets them apart. At Winchester, in addition to the 70 scholars, there were from the start 10 'commoners' and a further 60 men who made up the 'household', warden, teachers, servants and so on to make a total of 130. Meticulous record-keeping was one of the secrets of the success of the colleges, and are invaluable records today (Harwood 2005, 163-79).

A CHANGED CITY: THE COMMUNAL AND THE INDIVIDUAL

Detailed study of Winchester's buildings enables us to make some original suggestions about building in both stone and timber. Changes in the appearance, scale and functions of Winchester's building stock can be seen in the period leading up to the Black Death compared with the century or so that followed it.

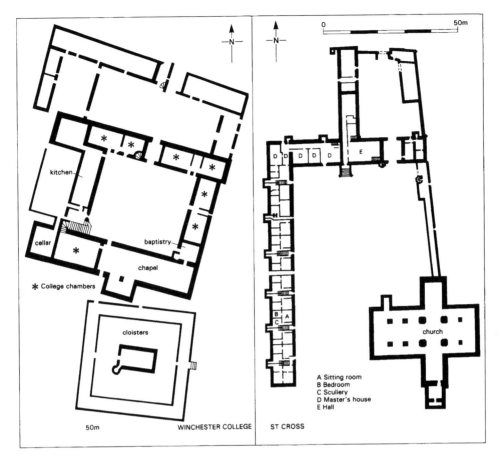

53 Winchester College by William of Wykeham (died 1404) and St Cross Hospital (accommodation for retired retainers of Cardinal Beaufort, died 1447) are exceptional examples of the late fourteenth- and fifteenth-century communal accommodation. Their plans are redrawn here to the same scale for comparison. *After Pevsner et al. (1967) and Winchester College Archaeological Society (1926); redrawn by Alexandra Gutiérrez*

Starting with the cathedral as an example at the grandest end of the scale: before 1348 it had, on our best guess, twin towers at the west end, which were demolished immediately prior to, or even during, the onset of the Black Death, leaving a fragment of the southern tower which still exists today. The triple porch we now see was created in the expensive Decorated style: work then seems to have ceased for a generation, perhaps because of the Black Death and subsequent plague, before work began again after 1370 when Bishop Wykeham completed the west front in the cheaper, plainer, mass-produced Perpendicular 'English' style. Meanwhile in the interior, the drum-piers of the Romanesque were cut back or rebuilt at this time to the style in which we see them today and the windows above adapted (54). At the great hall of the castle in 1349 Edward III altered the roofline so that Henry III's upstanding window reveals were dismantled and incorporated into an adapted structure (41a and 41b). Thus even the

54 Drawing by Professor Robert Willis (see 5a) demonstrating how the cathedral nave was adapted from Romanesque to Gothic either side of 1400. *Photograph John Crook*

wealthiest bishop and the king himself apparently made-do and mended, rather than built anew following the plague of 1348.

Similarly with timber-framed structures, dendrochronology (tree-ring dating) has shown a break in the tradition either side of 1348. Contrary to the traditional view that in crowded towns pre-1350 there were small buildings crammed gable on to the road, in Winchester at 35 High Street there was a huge Wealden house (the earliest such house so-dated in the country) parallel to the street; while not far up the road at 42 there was an exceptionally large timber-framed four storey house with a stone basement, its jetties supported in a pentice by upstanding timbers at ground level, dating to the first half of the fourteenth century and probably to 1347 or immediately thereafter. The Pentice as we know it today, dates to 1469-72, is made of much slighter timbers and has no comparable scale or basements. From this evidence it may be argued that the Black Death caused a break in vernacular building scale and style, as well as in stone building and style.

Finally, there is much more that is communal in Winchester following the plague: Mark le Fayre's George Inn has already been mentioned. Just to the east also on the north side of High Street is the Godbegot, another timber building round a courtyard with shops and other accommodation, created by the investment of the cathedral priory. The post-plague Winchester College, designed as a training-place to set up education for boys who would in time replace those clergy killed by plague, and the Hospital of St Cross, grandly rebuilt for retainers of Cardinal Beaufort before 1450 were also communal. Were these creations to draw together those who survived? All these structures, inns for estate managers and other folk visiting Winchester, and communal institutions for students and retainers, were for the administrative classes and clergy. Were these buildings part of a broad effort to manage the new social circumstances which prevailed post-plague? In the age of the Great Revolt of 1381 which threatened the authorities from within society, and French raids along the coast threatening from abroad, it is not surprising to find Winchester College and St Cross supplied with doughty gate houses, and the West Gate at Winchester rebuilt in like style at this time.

If there was a sense of the communal, this period after 1350 was also marked by the rise of the individual, again visible in Winchester. Among its manifestations are the life and career of Bishop Wykeham himself who comes into sharper focus than any of his predecessors. His chantry in the nave (communal area) of the cathedral priory has been derided as 'the privatisation of public space' (Binski). Wykeham's leading servants, those who created his buildings likewise come into the light: Simon Membury the mason, Thomas of Oxford the glazier, and Hugh Herland the master carpenter are not only known through copious documentation, but also are personally depicted in the east window of Winchester College chapel (if now only in nineteenth century copies of the fourteenth-century originals). A further, most striking, manifestation of the rise of the individual after the Black Death is seen at Wykeham's College where Warden Fromond made a bequest in 1420 to build a chantry, where prayers would be said for his soul. His chantry occupied the *entire* area of the cloister, the communal burial area. In the age of Chaucer and his clearly depicted pilgrims as seen in the Prologue to the *Canterbury Tales*

55 Fragment of the head of a bishop from the cathedral great screen, probably complete by 1476 and the sculptures in place soon afterwards. *Photograph John Crook; copyright Dean and Chapter*

of 1387, and succeeding generations, the new circumstances of wealth for those who were left behind by plague, contrasted sharply with the diminished income of landlords. Rents fell both for individual landlords and for institutions: falling incomes led to some redirection of resources and some jostling of individual against the community at large in the uncharted territory of post-plague Winchester.

7

RENAISSANCE WINCHESTER 1485-1660

The city changed appearance in the sixteenth and seventeenth centuries, and we have a better idea of developments from contemporary comments (p.14). The Reformation wrought the most significant change. Nunnaminster and Hyde Abbey (where large piles of rubble were left) were effectively demolished after 1539, as were the conventual buildings of the cathedral priory. The friaries disappeared, and the parish churches which had declined in numbers to some 26 in 1500 were to decline still further to 12 by 1600 through closure and amalgamation of parishes.

Tudor and Stuart mansions rose from the rubble of the friaries and monasteries and elsewhere in Winchester, especially in the suburbs, as land was more freely available in the wake of the Reformation. At Hyde, in the northern suburb, a residence appeared on part of the site of the Benedictine house, while the Mason family created a mansion out of Blackfriars within East Gate. Both these mansions have been demolished. Surviving large houses from this period include The Soke, in Chesil Street in the eastern suburb (see 3) and Moberly's (1571), in Kingsgate Street, south of the city walls.

The mighty medieval buildings suffered, especially in the Civil War, when there was severe damage to the castle, additional destruction at the cathedral to that caused by the Reformation and the virtual demolition of the bishop's palace at Wolvesey. The archaeological evidence at Wolvesey shows how the great stained-glass windows, for example, were collected together in the northern range and were broken up systematically, leaving concentrations of fragments of decorated glass and molten lead (Biddle 1990).

NATIONAL POLITICS AND LOCAL ADMINISTRATION UNDER THE TUDORS

The battle of Bosworth in 1485 was remote from Winchester but none the less affected the city. In 1486 Henry VII's first son, Arthur, was christened in the cathedral. The name Arthur and location for the christening further institutionalised the mythical ancient

56 Tapestry fragment approximately 2 x 1.5m (6ft 6in x 3ft 3in) showing the union of the roses of Lancaster and York, and traditionally associated with the christening of Prince Arthur, Henry VII's firstborn son, at Winchester in 1486. This and other tapestry fragments were apparently saved to Winchester College during the Civil War of the 1640s and two are displayed at the College. *Author's collection*

history of the city. The combination of King Arthur and Winchester's antiquity were grist to the mill of the fledgling dynasty. The baptism was a splendid affair with a procession (albeit only from the prior's lodging, now The Deanery, in The Close), a silver font brought from Canterbury, and the provision of rich cloth and tapestry hangings, some of which survive today in the possession of Winchester College (56). Around this time Henry VII's arms were carved in the cathedral and the remains of Saxon kings, including Cynegils an Ethelwulf, were placed in new chests set high on the presbytery walls replacing those made a century earlier, one of which survives in the Triforium Gallery. Such commissions boosted the standing of the new dynasty and encouraged people to think of the Tudors as successors to the Saxon kings who had contributed to Winchester's past greatness.

In 1522 the magic of Arthur and Winchester was once more activated, when Henry VIII welcomed Emperor Charles V to the city. In the Great Hall of the castle the Round Table was displayed, newly painted with the Tudor rose and bearing the names of the knights surmounted by a bearded Arthur – surely Henry himself, the first monarch known to have been bearded since Richard II over a century before (57 and Biddle 2000).

57 The Round table mirrors the union of the roses seen in 56. The table now hangs in the castle Great Hall. Although probably made c.1290 (see 43) it was not painted until 1522, in Henry VIII's time. Whether it was originally made for Winchester is uncertain, and some scientific evidence suggests it may have been made in the 1340s, the time that the Round Table building, recently partially discovered at Windsor Castle, was built by Edward III. *Copyright Hampshire Record Office 56M71/1056*

58 Bishop Gardiner (died 1555), Bishop of Winchester from 1531. Gardiner's sympathies were with Catholicism. After imprisonment during Edward VI's reign for his adherence to the 'old religion', he was reinstated and officiated at the marriage of Queen Mary and Philip of Spain in 1554. This portrait was recently returned to Winchester by King Juan Carlos of Spain. Gardiner's chantry chapel of 1556-8 in the cathedral was a striking Gothic structure decorated with Renaissance work – as symbolic of changing taste as his episcopate was of changing religion. *Photograph Peter Jacobs*

Winchester steered an unimpeachable political course during the remainder of the century and into the Stuart period. The mayor and burgesses were supportive of the Reformation, even taking part in the destruction of Swithun's shrine in 1538. But in 1554 they welcomed the Catholic monarchs Mary and Philip (58). In 1559 the city was awarded custody of the castle, and Queen Elizabeth visited on various occasions towards 1600.

A key to this success, particularly under Elizabeth and James I, lay in patrons and MPs. For example, Sir Francis Walsingham, a major figure in Elizabethan politics, was appointed High Steward of Winchester for life in 1582 at St John's House on the Broadway. At around the same time Thomas Fleming became Recorder and represented the city in the parliaments of the 1580s and 1590s. His fine house, The Soke in Chesil Street, survives and fragments of Renaissance decoration dated 1609 are still to be found there, a very rare connection between an individual and a decorative scheme in pre-modern Winchester (Lewis and Turle 2006, 215 and pl. 7). Fleming kept abreast of political change at the end of Elizabeth's reign and as Lord Chief Justice presided over the trial of Guy Fawkes following the gunpowder plot of 1605. He died after a party for his tenants in 1613.

Fleming's family and friends were staunch Protestants and assisted the city government in its attempts to contain Catholicism. Over 50 Catholics were listed for the Winchester area in 1581: over 50 per cent of the total for the diocese. Although one priest, John Slade,

59 The tomb at North Stoneham church of Sir Thomas Fleming, Recorder and MP for Winchester, and his wife Mary James, both natives of Newport in the Isle of Wight. Sir Thomas died in 1613 and Mary in 1614. *Photograph John Crook*

was executed in the city, the old religion appears usually to have been treated with disapproval rather than violence. This may have been because there were well-connected recusants such as Lady West, whose house in St Peter Street was found to contain missals, vestments and an altar in 1583 (she was assessed at 5*s.* in the tax of 1586), and was one of a number of Catholic households found within the walls and in the suburbs.

But Catholicism was an undercurrent (if a strong one): the mainstream of Winchester's politics and religion was in the hands of protestant clergy, gentry and merchants, loyal to queen and country. In 1588, while the country at large was embroiled in Armada-fever, Winchester received from Queen Elizabeth its reaffirmation of its governmental organisation in a royal charter. The city was to be henceforward governed by mayor, bailiffs and 'commonalty' (their supporting privileged burgesses), the 24, in whom were vested the right to hold property, to enjoy privileges and to have a seal. These arrangements were confirmed by her successors James I, Charles I and Charles II.

POPULATION AND SOCIAL STRUCTURE

By 1524 Winchester has declined to perhaps quarter or third of the size it had been in 1300 – perhaps 2000 or a maximum of 4300 inhabitants (James 1988). In 1524, 595 households were enumerated for taxation. Winchester's population rose to some 5270 around 1550, reflecting a surge in population nationally in the sixteenth century. There was a further rise to approximately 6240 in the early seventeenth century, comparing the evidence of the tarrage rolls of 1417 and 1603 (Keene 1985). Certainly in neighbouring Southampton the population rose to a peak of 4200 in the 1590s before falling back after 1600. Winchester may have mirrored those developments: the population in like manner falling back in the seventeenth century to perhaps fewer than 5000 during the Civil War. A variety of factors explain these fluctuations: including epidemics of plague, which continued until the 1660s, and the Civil War. In particular the phenomenal growth of London, from some 50,000 in 1450 to 575,000 to make it the largest city in Europe by 1700, adversely affected Winchester as it did all towns in central and south-eastern England from Tudor times onwards.

A wealth structure can be deduced from the 1524 lay subsidy – a new tax which caught the population unprepared to avoid it, and so provides a good account of wealth which can be analysed by grouping together those of the same assessment. It has often been argued that 30 per cent of the population was too poor to pay. In Winchester over 32 per cent were assessed at £1 – the lowest rate; a further 30 per cent pay the next rate, the £2-9 group. This gives a total of over 92 per cent whose goods and wages were valued at under £10. The £10-39 group amounted to over six per cent, and those valued at over £40 were just over one per cent of the population. The highest valuation in the city in 1524 was £60 – less than the £100 of several contemporary Southampton merchants. In broad terms the groupings within the tax bands in both towns were very similar. As it was a lay subsidy the clergy do not appear. At Winchester, as at Southampton, members of wealthy county families are found in the city towards 1500: thus by far the wealthiest person assessed at £10 in 1585 was Walter Sandes whose assessment compares starkly with the 14s assessment of wealthy William Symonds, three times mayor of Winchester (whose initials are found on a fine fireplace now set in the basement of 41 High Street). William's wealthy London-merchant brother Peter founded the Christes Hospital alms houses the following year (*60*; Davey 1991).

The Reformation removed ecclesiastical props on which the poor had depended for a millennium. The resultant development of the Tudor poor law made the relief of the poor and sick a lay responsibility. Apart from the administration of the poor rate, the city authorities administered funds which came to them through bequests. The outstanding example of this was the establishment in 1607 (after a 20-year delay) of Christes Hospital, Symonds Street (see *60*), for which the corporation purchased 100 loads of freestone from the ruins of Hyde Abbey.

Society in Winchester was turned upside-down during the Civil War of the early 1640s.

60 Christes Hospital, Symonds Street, established by Peter Symonds in his will of 1586 but not incorporated for 20 years, due to a family dispute. Many stones from Hyde Abbey, which had come into the hands of Symonds's step-father, Richard Bethell, were used in the construction of the almshouse, and some are visible here (lower courses and quoins, left). *Photograph and copyright Alex Turner*

A despondent former mayor, John Trussell, summed up the effects of the billeting in the city:

> Now what they sai they wowld doe they have done
> In making pore and ritch mens estate all one;
> The rytch no rent, the pore their howses gett,
> The ritch no mony have, the poore no meat ...
> Woe worth the while what shall become of mee
> When poore and ritch are thus in one degree.

ECONOMY AND ENVIRONMENT

Economic problems highlighted in the petition of 1452 did not evaporate with the arrival of the Tudor Age. The withdrawal of the cloth industry was already significant before 1485 and the city came increasingly to rely on its role as a market centre for the neighbouring hinterland.

The cloth industry struggled on in the city for another century after 1485, but continued to decline. In 1581, of the hundred wealthiest people assessed for tax, only nine were involved in the making, and only two in the retailing, of cloth. Retailing, food and drink trades, leatherworking and metal crafts dominate the other 90 per cent or so of the taxable top hundred. The continuing problems of clothworkers dominate calls for help from the city to central authority in 1618, 1622 and 1631, by which time the marginally less poverty-stricken of neighbouring 'hundreds' were called upon to pay relief for the clothworkers of The Soke. John Taylor, a traveller who visited in 1623 during these difficulties, though admittedly during the harvest in August, commented that he saw 'an ancient city, like a body without a soul ... I walked from one end to the other and saw not 30 people of all sorts'.

Transfer of property from religious to secular ownership was a key effect of the mid-sixteenth century Reformation on Winchester. However, the idea that ecclesiastical communal ownership simply gave way to ownership by lay individuals would be wrong. Certainly this happened in the case of Hyde Abbey, whose lands passed via Thomas Wriothesley to the Bethell family, who built a brick and stone mansion house on the site by 1570. Otherwise it was institutions, particularly the city government that gained property from the dissolved religious houses (*colour plate 12*). The city government in 1540 owned 109 properties (including 20 gardens), which generated 53 per cent of the corporation's income. By 1554 the number had increased to 183 (45 gardens) with a concomitant increase in income for the city. The city also inherited the sites of churches closed after the 1545 Act for the Amalgamation of Churches and classified as 'waste ground'. On the whole, in the century after 1450, property came to provide a significant proportion of the city government's income, which generally fluctuated between 40 and 60 per cent.

Economic links with the hinterland were a sufficient, if limited, base for the city's economy in times of peace in the sixteenth century. However, particularly during the Civil War of the seventeenth century, such links with the hinterland were easily broken. The Civil War was disastrous for the economy of Winchester. The market function, central to the economy of the city, was all but destroyed by the plundering of goods, carts and horses. The castle was cast down and Wolvesey destroyed.

CIVIL WAR: ROLE AND POLITICS

Winchester was important strategically in the Civil War as a bastion astride the great west road between the royalist west and the parliamentary south-east. The oligarchy and the Church gave it royalist leadership in the early 1640s. Divisions within the local gentry and between Winchester burgesses were thrown into stark relief by the choice between king and parliament.

One Winchester burgess was Sir William Waller, a parliamentary commander who defeated a royalist garrison of the city in 1642; and who allowed wholesale plundering of shops and general destruction. Another was Sir William Ogle, the chief royalist leader in the city. Ogle recaptured the city in 1643, was unable to prevent parliamentary looting for a second time in 1644 and was blasted out of the castle by Cromwell in 1645. Thereafter, the only overt connections to the war were the execution of a royalist who had plotted to 'spring' the king from imprisonment on the Isle of Wight, and a loyalist address to the king as he made what proved to be his final journey to London in 1648.

In 1651 a garrison was placed in the city to defend it against the threat of royalist resurgence inspired by the future Charles II. During the Interregnum there was a diminution of trade and its market function was curtailed. The city government which had supported the king – and whose members had been much criticised as self-seekers by John Trussell early in the 1640s – was replaced in 1649 by a pro-parliament group. This regime held sway until the Restoration.

RELIGION AND CULTURE

Whatever the decayed state of the economy in the later fifteenth century, the Church survived in a stable but reduced state in the final years of the fifteenth and the first four decades of the sixteenth century.

A regular programme of building took place at the cathedral during the last half-century or so of its existence as a priory. Under bishops Courtenay (died 1492) and Langton (died 1501) and their contemporary priors, Hunton and Silkstede, there were works in both stone and wood at the east end – work in the Lady Chapel and in Langton's own chapel. The embellishment of Langton's chapel by his successor, Fox, perhaps drawing on motifs from mainland Europe, was probably completed by 1510, and contained the first elements of Renaissance style in the city – among the earliest in England. This was followed by the construction of Fox's chantry chapel in 1513-18. Apparently originally entirely Gothic in its design by Thomas Vertue, the king's master mason, Renaissance elements crept in during construction. Fox went blind in later life, and used his chantry to hear mass. The decoration of the chapel with his motif, the pelican, towards the base of the structure may have enabled the unsighted prelate to feel his way into the chapel.

The main structural achievements in the cathedral in Fox's time (1501-28) were the walling in the presbytery and the provision in 1525 of Renaissance chests for the remains of Saxon worthies, now atop those walls. Both the presbytery walls and Fox's chantry chapels are built of Caen stone, imported via Southampton, and are, bar the detail, fine testaments to the final flourish of the Gothic at Winchester.

All this remains today. But adjacent to the Fox chantry stood the great shrine of St Swithun of 1476 (*colour plate 15*). Destruction of this focus for pilgrims for nearly half a millennium was concluded at 3a.m. on the morning of Saturday 21 September 1538. Silver valued at £1320, according to Wriothesley who oversaw the dismantling, was the main precious metal recovered. In 1539 the priory was dissolved and in March 1541 the new foundation of Dean and Chapter was established by letters patent from the king. Within the cathedral the new foundation was celebrated with a series of woodcarvings of the dean and chapter's stalls. The chapter consisted of 12 prebendaries, some of whom, like Dean Kingsmill, were recruited from former brothers.

The destruction of Swithun's shrine and the Dissolution of the monasteries not only had major economic effects but also topographic effects on Winchester. The cathedral priory, Nunnaminster (61), Hyde Abbey and all the friaries disappeared. Many buildings were demolished straight away, for example Hyde, whence stone, timber, slates, iron and glass from the church, cloister, chapter house, dormitory, frater, the hall and lodgings were taken for the king's use. At Nunnaminster careful archaeological excavation has shown contrasting activities by preservers and destroyers of the nunnery. While several tombs were carefully opened, perhaps by those wishing to preserve family remains or relics in the hope of a restoration of monasticism, others systematically destroyed valuables they found in the church. Melted and charred fragments of gold, pearls and semi-precious stones were recovered from hearths dug into the latest floor levels, probably by the king's men as they looted the nuns' church and smashed open tombs searching for valuables. A fragment of the structure may have survived until after 1600, if the evidence of Speed's map is reliable (WMSN 28, 1997; fig.2).

In common with the crown, its agents and speculators, and the city corporation, Winchester College also profited, gaining principally the lands of the Dominican and Franciscan friaries in the north-east sector of the walled city and certain lands beyond the walls derived from friary, chapel and chantry foundations. Away from the built up area of the city the dean and chapter and the bishop retained their lands (*colour plate 12*).

At the cathedral, the change from a priory to a regime based on a dean and chapter required adjacent properties for the new prebendaries. Thus the old prior's lodging was preserved as the Deanery, which it still is today. The building retains its impressive late medieval timber roof over the hall. Other significant survivals from the priory include a part of the kitchen (now incorporated into 10 The Close), the Norman pillars of the chapter house beside the south transept, and two notable timber-framed buildings: the 'Pilgrims' Hall' (probably the priory guest house) of c.1310, and the stables of c.1500, in the south of The Close (62).

The decline in the number of parish churches had slowed down in the fifteenth century, but the first half of the sixteenth century saw the closure of a further eleven out of the 57 of 1148. Bishop Fox carried out a rationalisation programme which closed most of this group, including St Mary in Tanner Street. St Mary's has been thoroughly excavated and the results show a building of flint rubble with some chalkwork, but, so far as is known, with little expensive ashlar work. Two churches, St Mary in the Cemetery (fragments of which survive to the west of the cathedral) and St Stephen, were closed as a direct result of the Reformation. Some of the once-grand churches of Winchester disappeared at this time, for example St Mary Kalendar (on the north side of High Street, opposite the east end of The Pentice), which was probably in ruins by 1554 when it was granted to the city. Some positive developments in parish churches did occur, however. In 1527 the wealthy suburban church of St John in The Soke was given 'seventeen messuages and quitrents', which added to its secure financial base founded on wealth from the St Giles Fair.

Right: 61 Reconstruction of Nunnaminster, the female religious house. Remains of which are displayed east of the Guildhall, south of High Street. Phases of the building from the Saxon to the late medieval are visible in the area displayed. Late medieval phases, which overlay the Saxon Eadburh's shrine are incorporated into the reconstruction shown here. Plans from limited excavations and use of known parallels are used here to re-create the minster. *After Winchester Archaeology Office; redrawn by Philip Marter*

Below: 62 Reconstruction, specially commissioned, of the cathedral priory at the time of the Dissolution, before 1538. The drawing takes account of surviving architectural fragments of the priory, results of excavations at St Mary in the Cemetery (left) and documentary research. *Drawn by Judith Dobie; English Heritage*

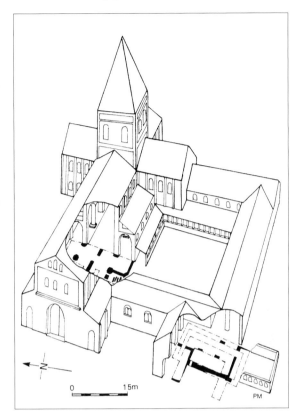

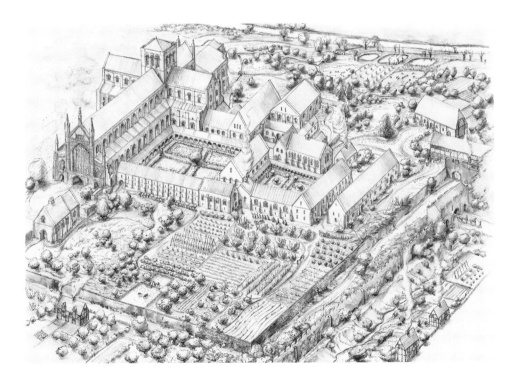

63 Tomb of Thomas Mason (died 1559). Fragments of this tomb, a cartouche 86 x 28cm (34 x 11in) and its male and female supporters, c.87 x 34cm (34 x 13in) are now in the Triforium Gallery. With Gardiner's chantry these were the only pieces of High Renaissance work in the cathedral. *Photograph and copyright Winchester Research Unit*

For the most part the century between the Reformation and the Civil War saw a continuing decline in both the decoration and numbers of ecclesiastical buildings in the city. Renaissance style, particularly in the context of the reformed Church, was less given to the statuary than the Gothic of previous centuries. This is most strikingly seen in the contrast between Bishop Fox's chantry of 1513-18, which has 55 groined niches, and Bishop Gardiner's chantry of c.1556-8, which has just three.

ROYALTY AND BISHOPS: 1550–1640

Among the reasons why Winchester was an appropriate place for the marriage of Mary Tudor and Philip of Spain in 1554 was its association with her uncle, Arthur, and his wife, Katherine of Aragon, who was also Mary's mother. The chair in which Mary is said to have sat during her marriage can be seen in the cathedral today.

Gardiner, bishop in 1531-51, and again 1553-5, confronted an uncertain future during the Reformation. A chapel established after his death by his successor, Bishop White, was intended as a chantry. But there is some doubt that it was ever completed – and it was the last such structure to be built in the cathedral. White's tenure was short: he was deprived of his bishopric and sent to The Tower.

Fragments of a remarkable Renaissance tomb of 1559 in the cathedral, which share ornamental features with Gardiner's chapel, have recently been reconsidered. This was the tomb, now largely destroyed, of Thomas Mason, whose father, Sir Robert, had been lay dean of Winchester from 1549-54 (63). However, not until the 1630s is the Renaissance theme once more taken up in the cathedral in the light of James I and Charles I's liberalisation of religion. The fine screen by Inigo Jones (now destroyed) adorned with bronze figures by Le Sueur, was the most significant element of the return of the Renaissance style which placed Winchester Cathedral 'once more in the forefront of English artistic endeavour' (Martin Biddle).

Undistinguished wooden portrait sculptures of kings James I and Charles I adorned the corners of the choir vault for almost two centuries from c.1635. These effigies survived the Civil War probably through their inaccessibility, but quantities of lead shot recovered from them after they were taken down suggest they may have been used for target practice by soldiers in the Civil War in an attempt to dislodge them (64).

The destruction wrought by the war, on the city and on the cathedral, was very considerable. Certain of the mortuary chests from Fox's screen were entirely destroyed, others severely damaged by acts of iconoclasm, which cut at the very roots of the discredited monarchy. Documents from the cathedral library were allowed to blow about unheeded. Some treasures such as the Arthur tapestries from 1486 were saved in Winchester College, but in terms of statuary, stained glass, fittings and documents the cathedral was wrecked as never before or since. The great twelfth-century bible survived both Reformation and Civil war: it was saved precisely because it contained the scriptures, the rock on which the reformed faith was founded. During the Interregnum the cathedral, like the city, lay quiet, awaiting whatever the future might bring.

64 This cathedral roof-boss of Charles I and Henrietta Maria was, like the portrait sculptures, out of reach of the Cromwellian soldiery. *Photograph John Crook*

8

'A GREAT DEAL OF GOOD COMPANY' 1660-1800

Winchester had fewer inhabitants for much of the late seventeenth and eighteenth centuries than in earlier periods. But the quality of life for those who remained there, where it can be tested, was comfortable and varied. In the period 1660-1700, Winchester was in the process of completing its transition from a declining former royal centre to a modestly successful administrative, market and social centre (Rosen 1975, 1981). Royal interest, exemplified by the planning and building of Charles II's palace on the site of the medieval castle in the 1680s, was both preceded and accompanied by a flurry of high-status housing for clergy and courtiers, a rebirth arising from Winchester's ancient dual status as both an ecclesiastical and a royal centre (Rosen 1981, 147). One indication of how things were changing is a rise in take-up and renewal of leases in the city, for example 130 in the period 1600-60, and 283 in the period 1660-1700; a sure sign that not only were the rich moving in but also of a boom in leasing by wider society (Mark Allen, pers. comm.).

Counting leases is one measure, but we can see the actuality of the material culture of the period both in surviving architecture and, through documents, in the content of those houses. Recent research has shown that domestic architecture and furnishings were developing rapidly, and expensively, in the decades before 1680 and continuing into the eighteenth century. Also, the highest growth in leasing is found after 1750. Probate inventory evidence suggests that some among Winchester's residents lived in real comfort enjoying clocks, mirrors, leather armchairs and feather beds: pictures hanging on the walls begin to proliferate and some had maps to decorate their houses, not only world maps, but, in 1746 one person had a map of Winchester on his wall. This group included clergy, wealthy merchants and that elusive group who were termed 'gent.' – not necessarily by themselves, but more significantly, for the student of social status, by their peers who drew up their probate documents (May 1998).

Thus a townscape of large and well-appointed residences emerges. The rebuilding of Wolvesey Palace by bishops Duppa (1660-2) and Morley (1662-84) after the Restoration followed the return of a resident bishop after the Civil War. The rebuilding drew on the

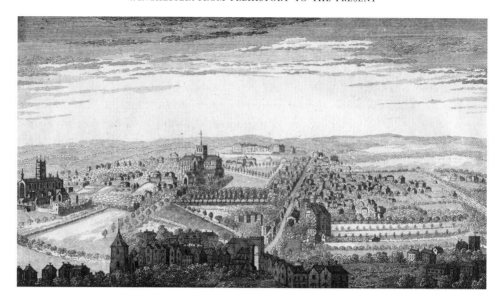

65 Ryland's East View of Winchester of about 1760, showing the northern areas within the walls, and the eastern suburb (right) even more depopulated than in the Bucks' view earlier in the century (see 3). *Author's collection*

ruins of the neighbouring medieval palace as a readily available quarry. Great houses were developed in The Close for the clergy; at first drawing on the available stone from the demolished conventual buildings as used at 9 The Close, then in brick as at numbers 1 and 11, an especially important house in the history of English architecture, with its *piano nobile* and servants' quarters banished to the semi-basement and into the eaves (May 1998; Crook 1984).

From the 1680s space within and outside the walls was in demand, for building large houses for courtiers at the time of Charles II's palace, and in the years following his death. These great houses were set in estates, some behind gates, such as Penton's House (*colour plate 13*). The eighteenth century saw a continuation of grand building, with red-brick mansions both within the walled area and in the suburbs, although the city walls were increasingly insignificant. Some 40 properties on High Street can be dated to the eighteenth century, but significant open spaces survived especially towards West Gate where a lithograph of *c*.1800 shows undeveloped areas both north and south of High Street (Cooper 2001; James 1993, no.79; compare also 65 and 74).

Visitors were divided about what they thought of the older monuments, though there were positive comments on the new grand houses. Some eighteenth-century visitors criticised the old timber-framed buildings. Plenty of fine seventeenth- and eighteenth-century domestic architecture is to be seen in the city. A good proportion of this is on a small scale, and provided dwellings for those who served and administered the large residences. Cottages and shops with brick frontages, such as those on Canon Street, at the Blue Dolphin Fish Bar on the Broadway and at 42 Chesil Street (the extraordinary pre-1300 survival), conceal earlier buildings, and incorporate timber frames behind their brick façades. Bricking up above the eaves, believed to prevent sparks from chimneys being sucked back under the eaves, became the health and safety mantra of the day after the Great Fire of London in 1666.

In premises such as 58 High Street, the former Jacob and Johnson's *Hampshire Chronicle* offices, and elsewhere in the city, such as in Kingsgate Street, there are bow windows, which some contemporaries saw as indications of shameful exhibitionism by people who wished to be seen! Where enlarged windows were added to medieval properties, for example at The Pentice in the High Street, there must also have been another motive – to provide additional light. Lighting the city was a priority for the pavement commissioners in the 1770s, and an expense for the taxpayers: by 1775 185 oil lamps lit the city from dusk until dawn, except during the six nights of full-moon (Cooper 2001, 142). The city boasts some eighteenth-century doorcases usually characterised by fine fanlights above, with particularly good examples in St Thomas and St Peter streets (Cooper 2001 and Appendices). All in all the city's pavement commissioners were waging war against filth by paving, and promoting health and safety through improved lighting and clearance of obstructions to encourage the free circulation of air.

POPULATION AND SOCIETY

The hearth tax of 1665, one of a series of ingenious taxes designed to raise money after the Civil War for a government with grand ideas but with little ready money, provides a basis for estimating a population of some 5900 in Winchester. The Compton religious census of 1676 (to discover numbers of Conformists, Nonconformists and Catholics) gives a somewhat lower figure of 3700 (James 1988; Hughes and White 1991, nos.229, 290-2). The hearth tax gives some clues to wealth distribution, and lack of it, in the city: 25 per cent of the households within the walls together with the eastern suburb were exempted on the grounds of poverty.

The difference in figures between 1665 and 1676 may reflect a genuine decline in population in the decade. The effects of the 1666 plague on the city constituted a major demographic setback, bringing about 'severe disruption' and were sufficiently severe for a decline of 25 per cent to be recorded in excise totals for the city between September 1666 and March 1667 (66) (Taylor 1984). The 1668 hearth tax commissioners cited Winchester as a city where plague had led to a decline in receipts.

Bishops' visitation returns between 1725 and 1788 provide useful indications of population size in this least-studied period of the city's history. Enumeration by incumbents of numbers living in their parishes in 1725 add up to just over 4000, of which 2758 lived in the parishes within the walls. This hints at a rise in the population of the suburbs. The incomplete returns for 1788 suggest an overall decline perhaps to between 3500 and 4000. There is no clear trend in 1788 of growth in the suburbs contrasting with decline within the walls.

Society in the city continued to be dominated by clergy, gentry and, more briefly, courtiers. Daniel Defoe, writing at about 1725, liked most of what he found:

THIS MONUMENT
Is Erected
By the SOCIETY OF NATIVES
On the very SPOT OF GROUND
To which the MARKETS were removd
And whofe Bafis is the very STONE
On which EXCHANGES were made
Whilft the City lay under the Scourge
Of the DESTROYING PESTILENCE
In the Year
Sixteenhundred Sixty Six.

66 Detail of the plague monument outside West Gate. Plague disappeared from Winchester after a final, serious, outbreak in 1666. *Photograph John Crook*

here is a great deal of good company; the abundance of gentry being in the neighbourhood, it adds to the sociableness of the place. The clergy also here are, generally speaking, very rich and very numerous. As there is such good company, so they are gotten into that new-fashioned way of conversing by assemblies.

However, he was (rather unjustly) critical of what he discovered of St Cross where the brothers were not 30 in number as he had expected but only 14, while the master lived in the style of the best gentlemen – a matter of complaint 'when public charities, designed for the relief of the poor are embezzled and deprecated by the rich to the support of luxury and pride'. The erroneous number of brothers at St Cross exemplify Defoe's tendency to be mistaken and to exaggerate for effect, for as contemporary visitations show, St Cross was indeed supposed to support only 13 men (Ward 1995, no.230).

THE RESTORATION AND POLITICS

The Restoration of 1660 was on the whole popular in Winchester and was in time to prove significant for the development of the city as we know it today. There was pain mixed with pleasure in 1662 when reforming commissioners ejected the 1649 city government on the grounds of disloyalty. Charles II granted a charter confirming previous reductions of the 'fee farm' or annual sum of compounded royal dues paid by the town to central government. At this time Charles gave the city the great Lely portrait of himself which hung for many years in St John's Rooms on the Broadway (see 5a), but now can be seen in the Guildhall.

Royal patronage was a two-edged weapon, for in 1684 Charles II called in the city's governing charter and refused to reissue it. Such relief as was felt at King Charles's death was short-lived as James II left the city without a charter until 1688 when he forced his own nominees on to the powerless corporation under the guise of reissuing a medieval charter. Ten weeks later in early December James, in desperate straits, reinstated the city's privileges and with them an Anglican council led by Thomas Wavell; soon afterwards the king was rejected by the country at large in the Glorious Revolution.

THE RESTORATION AND REBUILDING

On their return to the city after 1660, successive bishops found much needed to be done. Brian Duppa began by rebuilding Wolvesey between 1660 and 1662. His successor George Morley built enthusiastically: between them they spent £4000 on the bishop's palace. Morley also created the eponymous Morley College for clergy widows in 1674 on part of the vacant New Minster site to the north of the cathedral. It was at this time that another institution, Winchester College, began to modernise some of its building stock after some 350 years. The 1680s witnessed the building of the imposing 'School' for commoners.

The Restoration brought a spate of repair and building in the city. As Schellinks saw in 1662, the city walls were breached and the castle slighted. Wolvesey, once the greatest

Romanesque house in England, had, in the words of Defoe 'been ruined by that known church incendiary, Sir William Waller, and his crew of plunderers'. Elsewhere, buildings in the city had simply fallen into disrepair. Such was the case with the church of St Peter in Macellis on St George Street, which had not been a place of worship for at least a century before the Restoration and had become a collection of ruined walls, being 'no other than a very dunghill, a place of all manner of excrements and a loathsome, noisome nuisance to the parts of the city adjoining it'. This church was excavated in the 1950s.

Depopulation and decline left spaces in the city, but even in 1662 the High Street was in good order: 'the largest and best street for shops and houses', commented Schellinks. The 1664 bill was enacted for the creation of the Itchen Navigation, the culmination of a project mooted at various times over the previous 130 years, to connect Winchester to Southampton, and which eventually opened in 1710 (see Chronology). The great houses in Winchester, completed more speedily, included Sir Robert Mason's great Eastgate House, which boasted 16 hearths in 1665, and dominated the area north-east of High Street, formerly occupied by two friaries. Across the road, Abbey House flourished on the site of St Mary's Abbey. There were altogether a dozen houses each with the large sum of 10 hearths which, while not a certain indicator of wealth in every case, helps to define this group of large houses in the city. This group was swelled by canons' houses in The Close – there were nine such houses recorded with 10 hearths in 1674.

THE CAROLINE PALACE AND ITS LANDS

After attending the races at Winchester in 1682 Charles II decided to create an English Versailles in the city. He commissioned plans for an extensive palace on the medieval castle platform. The following year the foundations were laid and the building began to rise imposingly. The death of the king in 1685 halted the works (67). James II showed no interest in the project. The 138ha (342 acres) which had been acquired within and without the city for the project – partly for a grand vista from the palace to the cathedral – were blighted and the building activity in the city declined for a time due to uncertainty about the future.

In time the land began to seep back on to the market and the group of large red-brick houses was extended in the remaining part of the century and expanded in the eighteenth century. In 1705 there were 20 substantial houses in the city. Many of these large red-brick houses survive today both within the city and outside the walls. Among those from the seventeenth century are 11 The Close (1660s); Avebury House (1692); St Peter Street (for the Duchess of Portsmouth); Hyde House in the northern suburb; and Abbey House, of which only one wing now survives (for William Pescod, Recorder of the city). From the early eighteenth century fine examples include Serle's House and the former Southgate Hotel, Southgate Street, both probably from the second decade of the century, and 26/27 St Swithun Street of 1730 (see 3 and 65; John Crook and Pamela Peskett pers. comm.).

William Godson's measured map published in 1750 is the major cartographic source for the city before the nineteenth century (68). An album of his drawings of much the same date and marginal drawings on the 1750 map of some of the major structures

67a Charles II's palace, as it was eventually completed after his death, lacked much of the fine detail of Wren's design. The upcast of the Norman castle mound is seen in the foreground. The castle hall is to the right. *Author's collection*

67b Remains of the palace after the fire of 1894 (WCM PWCM 2084)

new, old and hypothetical are further useful visual materials. The east prospect of the King's House appears there as designed by Wren, and not in its complete form as built. Also drawn on the margin of the map are the old institutions – cathedral, college, great ('County') hall and market cross; almshouses – the old St John's on the Broadway and the new Morley College; and the town's centre of government – the new Queen Anne Guildhall of 1714 (*69*). Finally some grand houses including Wolvesey Palace and large private houses in the city are seen, the whole creation dedicated to the lay authorities: mayor, corporation and MPs of the city.

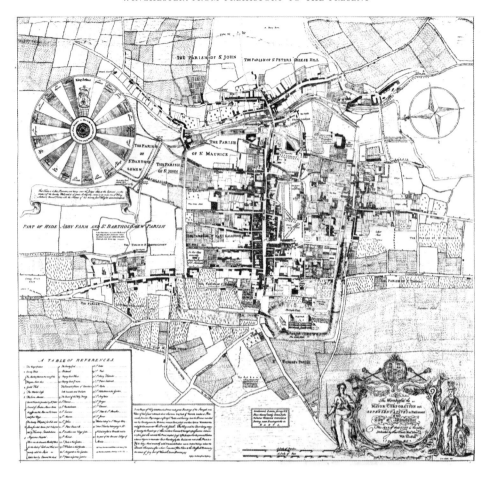

68 1750 map of Winchester by William Godson. The extensive areas of gardens both north and south (left and right) of the High Street indicate the continuingly depressed population of the city four centuries after the Black Death. *Author's collection*

ECONOMY

Building was not the only economic activity taking place in the 150 years which followed the Restoration. There is evidence of transport coming to the city and affecting the environment. In 1691 horse teams were banned from parts of the High Street on market days; in 1713 Kingsgate Street was widened to protect pedestrians from heavily laden carts. This may have been necessary because of the opening in 1710 of the Itchen Navigation from Winchester to Southampton, which terminated at Blackbridge Wharf near Winchester College, where cargoes such as coal were set on land. As it turned out the traffic was almost exclusively one-way from Southampton, partly at the insistence in the parliamentary bill of the 1660s that the trade should be limited to coal and 'the Norway trade'. Thus Kingsgate Street provided a comparatively level route for large, heavily laden carts unable to mount the steep Wharf Hill to get out into the city.

69 Queen Anne guildhall of 1714, from the marginal sketch on Godson's map of 1750. *Redrawn by Alejandra Gutiérrez*

In 1696 an estimated £20,000 worth of cheese was sold at the Magdalen Fair, which Celia Fiennes noted as a 'considerable', the event drawing 'a vast many of waines from severall parts especially from the West Country'. She noted hops as a prime commodity at the fair and hopyards on the banks of the ruined castle, below the new palace.

Wealthy gentry and clergy brought business (70): in 1676 there were 76 licensed victuallers. Ten years later the city far outstripped other towns in the county in a survey of stabling and was one of only six provincial towns in the country with stabling for more than 1000 horses. Medieval courtyard inns on the north side of High Street, such as 94 (The George, demolished in 1957) but noted for its stabling in 1647; 101-102, Godbegot and 157, the Coach and Horses where the eighteenth-century façade and courtyard-arch conceal an earlier timber-framed structure, testify to that provision of stabling and accommodation for travellers and visitors (Cooper 2001 for post-medieval histories of all properties on High Street).

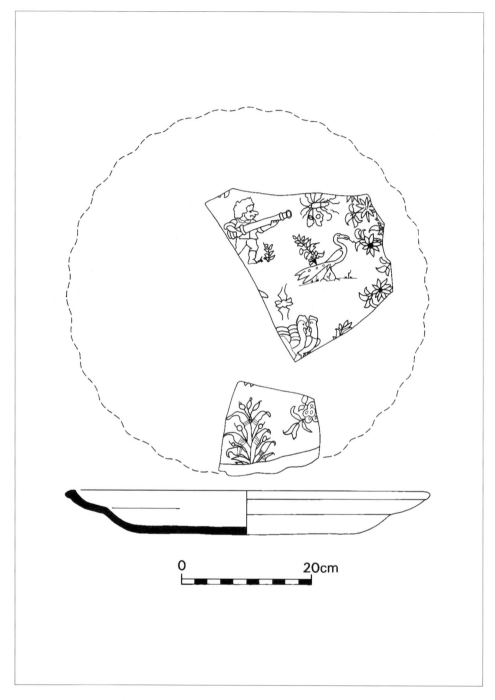

Above: 70 Fragments of a faience plate made at Moustiers in southern France *c*.1760 and excavated from the garden of 24 St Thomas Street. *After Matthews; redrawn by Alejandra Gutiérrez*

Opposite: 71 The city from the south engraved by William Westall for *Great Britain Illustrated* published *c*.1830. It shows a lock on the canal with the former palace (barracks) in West Hill and the cathedral in the valley below. *Author's collection*

In 1704, 90 shops were assessed within the walls supplying the rising population with food and services. However, the flurry of economic activity before 1700 was perhaps beginning to fail when Daniel Defoe recorded of Winchester 'here is no manufacture, no navigation' (inaccurate in the latter assertion, unless his publication of 1725 referred to a visit before 1700) although he found the society of the city agreeable. Thereafter there was, perhaps, a gradual improvement, most strikingly the creation of a silk-mill which employed 300 people by 1800 in the east of the walled area and, from the point of view of the building trades at least, the creation of a fine hospital and successive prisons and, from the steep rise in leases after 1750, housing for all ranks of society.

RELIGION AND CULTURE

In 1721 it was remarked that clergy occupied the best houses in Winchester. In 1735 four Cambridge gentlemen on tour noted the great reduction to nine of the number of parish churches. It was also noted that Morley's once-splendid palace at Wolvesey had run to ruin because, it was suggested, his successors perhaps thought it 'too magnificent for Apostolick men to live in'. However, there was a striking contrast between the wealth and residences of the bishops and senior clergy, and the stipends of the parish clergy, who fell in social standing as their incomes failed to keep up. This was partly due to the failure of the hierarchy to manage effectively their great estates. Even builders and philanthropically-minded bishops such as Duppa and Morley – although they did more than most – did little to raise the stipends and therefore the quality of life of their parish clergy (Thomson 2006).

This polarisation in the Church of England arose from a variety of a variety of factors. A number of the bishops in the eighteenth century were mostly older men, appointed to Winchester in their declining years, and who were not keen either to live there or to take an active role in the diocese: Willis was 60, Hoadly 58 and John Thomas 64. Hoadly (1734-61), notorious among bishops of Winchester for his lack of interest in the diocese, on becoming bishop displayed odious nepotism in the ordination and immediate appointment of his son John as Chancellor of the Diocese, a position he held from the 1730s until his death in 1776, while also being rector of St Mary's Southampton, of Overton and of Wroughton Wiltshire, to which he added the Mastership of St Cross from 1760 to 1776. Brownlow North (died 1820), brother of the Prime Minister Lord North and appointed bishop in 1781 was, like young John Hoadly, the beneficiary of nepotism also at a comparatively young age, being made bishop of Winchester at 40. In turn he promoted his own son Master of St Cross, creating more scandal even than Hoadly had done (see below, p.156). He spent the second half of his life as Bishop of Winchester, but little of it in the city. He spent a good deal of time and money restoring Farnham Castle but at Winchester he demolished the south and east wings of Wolvesey.

Anglicanism required reconstructing and re-establishing after the Interregnum, and these reforms were to an extent blown off course by the increased popery at court, especially in the later years of Charles II's reign and into the reign of James II. Eighteenth-century bishops instituted visitations of their dioceses to monitor activity, demanding written replies. Despite the almost continuous amalgamation of parishes since 1350, there remained a number of tiny parishes in Winchester as late as 1788 when the incumbent measured St Mary Kalendar parish at 1335 x 450ft and St Maurice at 1170 x 1365ft. Both were left to the same curate, while in the equally tiny St Michael's parish in the southern suburb, where there was 'no parsonage house, barn or out house', a curate held sway in 1765 as the rector 'is in Minorca' (Ward 1995, nos.425, 609-10). References such as these indicate some of the problems confronting bishops at this time: the unreformed nature of parochial organisation – there had, for example been no church in St Mary Kalendar for centuries, hence the running together of the parish with St Maurice, where a church was extant, but which might appear at first sight as idle plurality on the part of the rector. Small parishes and lack of accommodation, as at St Michael's, were issues that required addressing by the authorities as they re-established the national church in an era when nonconformity and Catholicism were allowed by act of parliament after 1689.

Catholicism became an increasingly significant feature of the religious life of the city after the Restoration. A Catholic graveyard, still in existence beyond West Gate, was opened soon after 1660, Charles II's Catholic queen brought her chaplains and the Duke of York encouraged Catholicism in Winchester before he became James II and mustered a Catholic council in the dying days of his reign. As early as 1676 the Compton Census showed a concentration of Catholics in Winchester, which while not great was 'certainly large enough to permit a sense of group solidarity'. With royalty involved the penal laws were ignored in Winchester and Catholics gained in confidence, several substantial families and poorer people as one Anglican clergyman put it 'seduced by rich

72 The eighteenth-century Milner Chapel. A fine Gothic Revival interior, and home of Catholic worship in the city. *Author's collection*

Roman Catholicks … go to their mass'. But the 'discreet zeal and moderation' preached by the Anglican Reverend Brereton, to his great indignation, led only to his being 'abused, insulted and persecuted by the prevailing party of rich Papists who instigate the common people to revile me in the street'. Brereton went so far in 1725 as to say that, to his great consternation, he found a 'predominant spirit of popery among many of my parishioners'. However, Catholics made such a great financial contribution to the city that the mayor in 1720 refused to comply with a demand from the bishop to expel them. By 1800 not only were there Benedictine nuns established in St Peter Street and French priests at the former palace, but the fine Gothic Revival Milner Chapel in St Peter Street (*72*) which provided a new focus for the old religion in the city. The returns to the Bishop in 1788 confirm a growth in Catholic numbers, and that they were accepted as part of parish life in the city (Ward 1995, xxiv-v, nos 229-237).

As for recreation, the attraction of the races which alerted Charles II to the city's possibilities for escape from plague, for rest and recuperation, was only one element in the cultural offerings available at Winchester. Restoration plays were very popular and bands of players came and performed in the hall over the meat market after 1660. However, early in the eighteenth century certain citizens of Winchester successfully lobbied the city government for a ban on players as they would be 'very prejudicial and corruptive to the youth, servants and other inhabitants' of the city. But this Puritanism could not be sustained indefinitely, and Samuel Johnson brought the Salisbury players to the city in 1763 and they came regularly thereafter. Johnson's friend Thomas Warton, member of the Hampshire book club, professor of Poetry at Oxford, Poet Laureate (1785) and brother of Joseph Warton, Headmaster of Winchester College from 1755, contributed for many years to intellectual life in Hampshire and Winchester. The location of the Winchester theatre, above the meat market, inspired the poet Warton to a humorous poetic reflection – perhaps not his most profound or literary poetic confection – on the Winchester theatre, above, and the shambles, beneath. This took the form of a prologue to Otway's play *The Orphan* (1680):

> Then kindly listen while the Prologue rambles
> From wit to beef, from Shakespeare to the shambles!
> Quick the transition when the curtain drops
> From meek Monimia's moans to mutton chops

This foreshadows the end of the tragedy in which Monimia and her devoted, but misinformed, twin-suitors all lie as dead meat upon the stage.

The new Winchester theatre was built in 1785 and opened with *The Rivals*. The ceiling of floating clouds was painted by William Cave, the Winchester artist, and the play season coincided with the annual St Swithun's day race meeting in July (Ranger 1996, 1). It continued until 1861 when it was finally closed, and part of the building survived until the 1980s when it mysteriously 'collapsed' during work on the site for a major development. Its legacy is a structure which includes some architectural features copied from the original theatre building. The closure of the theatre may have inspired the local thespians photographed by William Savage in 1872 (see p.143).

Private recreation in the form of the book and music business has been sampled and shows a variety of materials produced and distributed in Winchester in the second half of the eighteenth century, and a number of circulating libraries. One printer (perhaps an underestimate), Colson, was at work in the city in 1710, although there were only some four printers in Hampshire by 1750; but by 1800 there were five, half as many as in Portsmouth which had the most by far. John Wilkes of Winchester, who printed the *Hampshire Chronicle* from 1778-83, also printed a wide variety of other materials, some 20 books in the 1780s and 90s (fewer than the 30 books printed by James Robbins in the city at the same period, and which included Milner's *History* of the city). Wilkes appears to have specialised in books about trials and murders, notably that of James Aitken ('John the Painter'), the incendiary at Portsmouth dockyard who was tried at Winchester in 1777, and which had a wide distribution, as did *The Genuine Trial of the Honourable Augustus Keppel* (1779), in the production and distribution of which he was also involved. At a local level he sustained himself by producing books for authors who would pay, for example *A Treatise fully Explaining the Art of Brewing in the best Manner* (1783). Like his successor Thomas Blagden as printer of the *Hampshire Chronicle* to whom he sold his business in 1783, Wilkes ran a circulating library and in 1782 made available *Bell's Poets* not only from his own premises, but via a series of agents across the county and into Sussex. Blagden, however, was a stationer, who sold paper, quills, sealing wax, penknives and much else besides. John Burdon had been running a bookshop in College Street, Winchester (now Wells's) for over 40 years in 1800 (Oldfield 1983).

73 Parchment Street Hospital. Founded in the eighteenth century, the hospital was at the end of its life when this picture was taken *c.*1865 (WCM PWCM 3625)

Wilkes opened a music shop in Winchester in 1779 selling music by established composers such as Haydn, Mozart and Scarlatti as can be seen from a list of his musical wares printed in the *Hampshire Chronicle* in 1780. He also aimed at a wider market with 'Hook's Vauxhall Songs 1779', 'Six new favourite minuets performed at Bath' and 'a Variety of several Thousand favourite Songs, Duetts, Minuets, Marches etc' as well as instruments and musical supplies '… Roman and Italian strings, violin bows, bridges … and every other article in the Instrumental Way'. There were tutorial publications such as 'Music made easy', indeed 'any Pieces of Music not in this Collection, on Three days notice' (Oldfield 1993). Another event hints at a rich musical scene at Winchester at that time. Also in 1779 a performance took place of the polymath James Harris's *Daphnis and Amaryllis*, set by the author to music by Handel, perhaps the last public performance in the librettist's lifetime, as Harris died the following year (Dunhill 1995).

Improved lighting at home and in public places was necessary for reading books and newspapers and for performing music. This was provided for daytime activity by the increasing size of windows and the bow-windows, referred to above. In institutional buildings, a few splendid multi-branched chandeliers, which must have brightened activities considerably, have survived, dating from the *c.*1700-50, although not now in their original positions: (formerly) at St Lawrence church (1700), in Winchester College 'School' (1729) and a donation to the cathedral by Dean Cheyney (1756) (Sherlock 2006).

POLITICS, ECONOMY AND GOVERNMENT AFTER 1700

In 1716 the city council was provided with a new guildhall centrally on the south side of High Street. It is adorned with a statue of the donor, Queen Anne (see 69); its curfew bell still sounds at 8p.m. The eighteenth century was quiet in Winchester, which no doubt much commended itself to the citizens, compared to the upheavals, hopes and disappointments of previous centuries. Corruption in politics and struggles between great county families such as the Paulet dukes of Bolton (at Abbotstone and Hackwood) and the Brydges and Chandos (Avington), characterised the century. However competition did provide certain spin-offs, such as the clock on the Guildhall given by a Paulet in the response to the statue of Queen Anne provided by a Brydges. Residents similarly vied with one another, both by building – such as Pescod and Penton either side of the Broadway – and by packing the council with freemen.

If the politicians of Winchester were not in agreement about what they did want for the city, they were agreed about what they did not want: disease (73), dirt (evidenced by paving commissioners who began work in 1771) and a proposal for the establishment of a massive penal institution at the King's House (as an alternative to transportation), which was effectively opposed in 1785. The eighteenth century closed with much evidence of an improved infrastructure for the city, which enabled Winchester to grow once more in the coming century. Essentials for the city to re-emerge as a populous county town were in place: a diverse retailing base, inns and alehouses and even, in silkweaving, a fledgling industrial activity.

The last quarter of the eighteenth century saw a considerable revival in the city's fortunes, hints of which are seen above in the businesses pursued by Wilkes and Blagden, and can be seen in *Sadler's* the first Hampshire directory of 1784 which lists a distinctive group of leatherworkers, including shoemakers, silk traders, as well as other luxury traders such as Blagden the bookseller and china makers. The emergence of the silkweavers and the burgeoning of public building works: the pavement works, the bridewell, gaol, markethouse and theatre gave an industrial edge to the city, raising up builders and carpenters as they had flourished in the later medieval building boom, to balance against the professionals. For example, 20 attorneys were listed in 1784, with insurance agents, medical people in the County Hospital (which offered medical relief and also opportunities for research, as when the bodies, for example of four black murderers in 1796, were sent there for dissection after hanging) and teachers, for example at Winchester College (Allen 1999, 40 citing Stedman 1979; Spence 1992).

9

'NO ONE CAN BUILD SUCH PLACES NOW' 1800-1900

Winchester grew in population in the nineteenth century: indeed, the city almost tripled in size. Rising rural population coupled with low wages and increasing mechanisation encouraged mobility of population. The agricultural Swing riots of 1830 were especially bitter in Hampshire villages. As a city where courts were held and where with both a county bridewell and a county gaol, Winchester was a focus during and after these riots of 1830. The city magistrates – who set the rate for the county – contributed to the onset of the riots by the 'humiliating and meanspirited' measures of lowering labourers' allowances. The rioters threatened to march on the city and burn down the Bridewell. In the end, however, the heavy hand of the law prevailed and the Hampshire rioters were dealt with especially severely in the trials at the great hall in the city where 101 were sentenced to death (three were executed) and 117 transported to Australia (Kent 1997). By the time Winchester underwent political reform after 1832, including the reform of the poor law, some of rioters were on the other side of the world.

The growth of Empire and the proximity of Southampton docks made the barracks a busy place, and the railway, which arrived from Southampton in 1839 and was opened through Basingstoke to London in 1840, provided a dedicated siding for the soldiers (Allen 1999). This increased mechanisation of troop transport was to culminate in 1914-18 when unimaginable numbers of troops were moved rapidly through the city to the western front and beyond. Meanwhile, Hampshire was, for example, a prime base for the Zulu war of 1879 and at least one hero of that war, Lt Col. Tongue of the South Wales Borderers, is among those buried in the West Hill cemetery. The Church of England was revitalised in Victoria's reign and the city was provided with a number of fine new churches, their Gothic Revival style echoing the medieval cathedral and Winchester College (*colour plate 18*).

74 The West Gate in the early twentieth century, scarcely changed since the fourteenth century, and a survivor of the historic gates of the city. The open space within the city walls is indicated by the distance between the arch and the nearest house on the south side of High Street. *Author's collection*

POPULATION AND SOCIETY

In 1801 the first decennial census found 6069 people in Winchester, a substantial rise from the maximum estimate of 4000 for 1788. In 1831 the population was 9212, on the eve of the cholera outbreaks that were to plague the country for some 30 years, but which had ceased to be a problem in Winchester by 1871. It was the enumerations of 9889 in 1841 and 12,402 in 1851 which were the first figures to match and then exceed 11,625, the highest projection for the Middle Ages. After 1850 the city grew steadily by 500–1500 per decade to reach 19,670 in 1891 (Allen 1999; Allen and James 2006). While this growth was exceptional in terms of Winchester's growth in the previous millennium, in terms of regional and national growth it was small. Southampton, for example, had a similar population to Winchester's in 1800, but was four times the population in 1851, and expanded exponentially thereafter to dwarf Winchester by 1901 (James 1983; Allen 1999).

The decennial censuses provide useful snapshots of the population. The 1871 census for Winchester has been studied in most detail and is available for computer analysis with a discussion of how it was compiled and some analysis of its content, sampled here. In 1871 the population was 17,301, somewhat more than the 16,366 within in the boundaries of the municipal borough. Institutions contained the largest groups in the city: 800 men of the 46th Foot (South Devonshire Regiment) and 170 Hampshire militiamen in the barracks; 347, of whom 90 per cent were men, in the prison, with a further 45 women in the Battery House; Winchester College had over 326 pupils on census night, supported by 77 servants and another 40 or so masters, their families and visitors; there were 160 people, largely men, in the workhouse and 115 people (90 patients) in the hospital. Each group contains a host of interesting individual life details, of whom the most exotic was maybe 'The Prince of Wales' a 40 year-old native of Africa and former Royal Navy seaman, languishing in the prison. Many of the service people were natives of Hampshire, but a significant proportion, 315 soldiers and 22 officers, were natives of Ireland (Allen and James 2006).

The population was generally rather young, with an average age of 28 among women and just over 26 for men. The gender split in the city overall, including the barracks, was at first glance almost equal: 98 men to 100 women, near the national average of some 49:51. Without the men of the barracks the ratio is an unusual 87:100, a reflection of the high number of institutions, service and professional households in Winchester with their armies of servants. There were over 1000 servants in 1871, described in a myriad 285 different ways. Of the gender groups as a whole at Winchester in 1871, fewer than five per cent were male domestics while 55 per cent were female domestics.

Significantly, if predictably, there was a good showing in the professional group, most numerous were teachers (175 consisting of a wide range from the head of Winchester College to pupil teachers), followed by those with a religious occupation (94), lawyers and their clerks and stationers (44); there were numerous shopkeepers, publicans and other established urban occupations among the 50 per cent of those listed who provided an occupation. Among the smaller occupational groups were 13 photographers, plying a trade only invented within the previous generation, and notably containing the famous Winchester photographer William Savage, whose studio was behind his fancy-goods shop at 58 (renumbered from 97 in 1869) High Street. Savage, a native of Winchester, photographed most of the city's major buildings, local people such as Hugh Wyeth (1872) a member of the first local Dramatic Society, of which Savage was also a member, in a costume of Iago in Shakespeare's *Othello*, the Barings at Northington Grange, and even Oscar Wilde. In 1871 his two daughters, in their 20s, assisted him in his work (Allen and James 2006; www.winchestermuseums.org for a sample of his photographs including Wyeth and WMSN 51, 2005; *52*).

The geographical origins of the population were largely local: 67 per cent born in Hampshire, of whom 37 per cent (including children of immigrants) were born in Winchester. Migration patterns were traditional, largely from the locality: some three-quarters of the population were born within the city, or within a day's walk of Winchester. However, that leaves a significant quarter of the population which came from further afield: 10 per cent from counties bordering Hampshire, with the general migration pattern of the city from west and north, the largest group from the east being four per cent who had been born in the London area, including a significant proportion of professional people. The three per cent of Irish have already been mentioned, and there were a number of native Scots, who, like the Irish were mostly soldiers or otherwise labourers and hawkers. Over 250 people were born abroad: the largest group, some 120, born in the 'East Indies' and India, some the children of colonial staff, missionaries and teachers, and some 40, mainly born in France, from continental Europe. There were 21 native Australians and 20 born in the West Indies and the 16 born at sea remind us of the ceaseless travelling that managing Empire and far-flung family life entailed in nineteenth-century society. The mysterious 44 people who professed not to know their birthplace remain a puzzle: we shall never know whether they were concealing their origins, or had genuinely lost track of their origins (Allen and James 2006).

ADMINISTRATION AND POLITICS

Winchester's role as a county town where courts were held and prisons were sited, is clear after 1800: a 'New County Bridewell', as it was termed on a map of 1805, in the northern suburb at Hyde, was supplemented within the ancient walled area by the architect George Moneypenny's 1805 extension of the gaol in Jewry Street, which was briefly renamed Gaol Street (Ball 1818). This unenticing appellation was abandoned and 'Jewry Street' was revived in 1830. By 1850 another gaol was erected on West Hill. This is still in use today. The great hall of the medieval castle, where trials had long been held, was refenestrated by O.B. Carter *c*.1850 together with the adjacent Grand Jury Chamber (Freeman 1991).

Winchester was rarely, if ever, at the centre of political reform, although the 1832 Great Reform Act forced the city to take action. The Commissioners reported in 1835 and found Winchester city government not at all to their liking. The column headed 'Whether any accounts and how kept' says 'Very ill kept', while elsewhere in the Winchester administration they found 'mismanagement and misappropriation to a considerable extent … At Winchester, the management has been actually taken from the Corporation in consequence of notorious malversation' summed up by one local historian as the activities of a 'corrupt and inward-looking' Corporation (Commissioners *Report* II, p.48 cited in Crossley 2003, 38-9; Carpenter Turner 1992, 126). Even if the commissioners' claims were true, and there is some evidence they were not, reforms worked through very slowly (Crossley 2003). From an administrative and architectural point of view the major changes came towards the end of the century with the building of the neo-Gothic guildhall adjacent to the Broadway in 1873 and with the creation of the Hampshire County Council in 1888, with offices based around the former castle site.

THE RAILWAYS

The London and Southampton Railway (later the London and South Western Railway), after nearly 10 years of planning and building, opened in the city from Southampton in June 1839. Unparalleled earthworks were needed to bring the railway to Winchester

75 Didcot, Newbury and Southampton Junction Railway: cutting in progress at Chesil, in the eastern suburb. The railway reached Winchester from the north in 1884 (HRO 85M88/13)

from Basingstoke (opened 1840). Expensive though these works were this main line from London was likely to be profitable, if any railway through Winchester was ever to be. There were some local investors, but on the whole the money came from London and from Manchester in particular, from the very heartland of the development of industrialisation. The station was established at the north-west corner of the old city defences, after an initial plan to drive the line through the old walled area near Staple Gardens, had been defeated, but not before a good deal of building – the Corn Exchange in Jewry Street, for example, had begun in a burst of ill-judged anticipation. However, Jewry Street has remained the main thoroughfare from the commercial area to the railway station (Allen 1999; Freeman 1991).

The economy and growth in size of the city led to the arrival of a second railway, the Didcot, Newbury and Southampton Junction Railway. Winchester did not feature in the title of the railway: Southampton men provided the commercial impetus for this railway company competition, alarmed at the power of the L.S.W.R. who also owned the docks there (Temple Patterson 1975). Winchester's dark, Chesil Station, its marginal site forced almost literally into the chalk hillside and approached by an expensively constructed tunnel, opened in 1885 in the eastern suburb. By coincidence this was the year in which the sixth turnpike had been freed from toll in the city: five others had been freed and the tollhouses disposed of in the 1870s. However, the time was not propitious for the new railway. Nationally there had been a severe recession over the previous decade, locally there were financial problems among the investors leading to acrimony and infighting. The investors were not the substantial entrepreneurs from the wealthy north-west of England as with the L.S.W.R. There were also engineering difficulties: the D.N.S.R was linked to the Great Western which partly ran on broad gauge. All this contributed to delays until 1888-9 when the extension of the railway across the flood plain of the Itchen, south of the city to Shawford, was achieved. By this time funds had been exhausted and investors had to face the unpleasant and humiliating necessity of linking to the L.S.W.R. to complete the connection to Southampton. Contemporary photographs show the major scale of the cutting and tunnelling which were required to create the railway in the area of Chesil Station (75 and Allen 1999). A brief period of competition of horse-drawn vehicles with railways ensued, but the first motor-car was on the road by 1900.

The economic effects of the railways on business and industry in the city have been subjected to recent analysis in which the first discovery was that the population of Winchester was already rising – by 45 per cent – in the decades between 1801 and 1831, before the railway arrived (Allen 1999, 36). However, it is plain to see in contemporary trade directories and newspapers that the railway enabled a growth in numbers of tourists who came to visit the city and other attractions nearby. Road transport, often provided by hotels and inns, met trains; printed guides and other publications, such as postcard views of the city, became readily available in the closing years of the century. Local carriers gained from the railway as they plied between the railway's stations and commercial premises. However, not every business benefited from the coming of the railways. Trade directories show how long-distance stage coach travel, for example to London, was immediately eclipsed, with a predictable knock-on effect on hotels, their ostlers and associated activities even if the rooms were now taken by rail-travellers.

GEORGIAN AND VICTORIAN BUILDINGS

In 1800 much of the city was devoid of inhabitants. Cole's map of 1805 shows large areas of the Brooks, north of High Street, as gardens with orchards on the western sloped within the walls. The northern, southern and eastern suburbs, however, were well stocked with properties but there is nothing much to the west. The brooks which flowed along the middle of the three Brook streets were open to the sky, with a number of medieval timber-framed houses still standing adjacent to them, as Samuel Prout's watercolour of 1813 shows.

This environment changed with ever increasing rapidity during the century. In particular the area of the Brook streets was developed beginning in the early years of the century and, as plots were bought up and tightly packed with red-brick housing, accommodated the increased numbers of inhabitants enumerated in the censuses. One example of this is illustrated by James Pulsome and his family who began buying up plots in the late eighteenth and early nineteenth centuries. The greatest period of growth in building was in the 1830s, and tenement blocks such as his eponymous

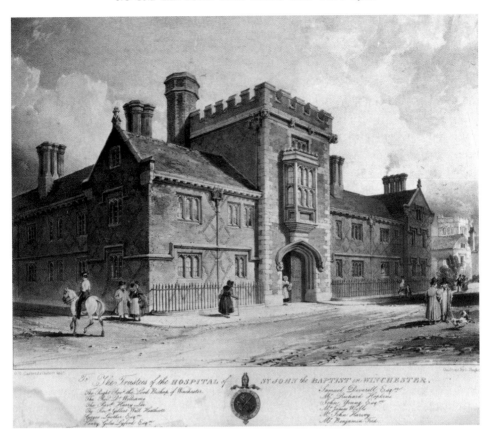

76 St John's Hospital, South. Owen Carter's fine lithograph of Garbett's buildings of 1833. *Author's collection*

'Pulsom's' buildings developed rapidly in the Brooks (Allen 1999; Cooper 2001). At the top end of the scale change was wrought by the creation of impressive buildings visible today, designed by a number of talented architects: the prison, Jewry Street, 1805 (Moneypenny); St John's Hospital and almshouses, South, High Street, 1833 (Garbett) (*76*); and the Corn Exchange, now the library, Jewry Street, 1838 (Carter). Other works were by H.C. Browne (died 1853) and his son-in-law Thomas Stopher.

Stopher created many buildings in the city in brick and flint, often with some structural and/or detail timber, especially on corner sites – The Old Dolphin (High Street/St Thomas Street; The Talbot Inn (High Street/Staple Gardens); The Green Man (Southgate Street/St Swithun Street); The Crown and Cushion (now demolished, Jewry Street/North Walls); and many others including the De Lunn buildings opposite the Theatre Royal in Jewry Street which show his lavish use of timber and steeply pitched roofs. The stone of the Gothic Revival churches of the early and mid-nineteenth century was followed by vernacular, less authentic architecturally in its re-creation of medieval and early modern buildings than stone of the churches.

77 Garnier Road pumping station, opened in 1875, contributed to the alleviation of sewage problems in the city (WCM PWCM 9985)

AMENITIES

Winchester has always been plagued by dampness and poor drainage. It was these problems which led, for example, to the relocation of the hospital from Colebrook Street to Parchment Street. This was a wise move as it placed the hospital slightly further from the river, but more symbolically it moved the hospital from the ecclesiastical south-eastern quarter of the city to the 'people's' area north of High Street, thereby symbolising the church's withdrawal from the medical function it has championed in the Middle Ages. No real progress was made towards a solution to the drainage problem until, in 1844 the whole matter of drainage was opened up by the corporation's sanitary inspector when it developed into the acrimonious 'muckabites' dispute in which the townspeople (who were ratepayers) opposed the improvements, while the institutions (exempt from rates) were in favour! Among the telling arguments adduced to support the proposals for change was that in well-drained towns life expectancy was 58. It was only 50 in Winchester and in St Peter Chesil parish, near the river in the eastern suburb, it was only 42. Indeed no cholera deaths were recorded west of St Peter Street, which marked the northern boundary of the overcrowded and insanitary Brooks area. The Brooks themselves were used for sanitation, and contributed to the spread of water-borne cholera (Boorman 1990; Allen 1999).

78 Following vigorous debate, spearheaded by Florence Nightingale among others, The Royal Hampshire County Hospital (foreground) was designed by William Butterfield and admitted its first 16 in-patients in 1868. In the background the County Gaol is seen, its cartwheel shape echoing Pugin's nightmare of a nineteenth-century institution (see *4*). Thomas Stopher (senior) was involved in the design of the prison in 1847: it was occupied by 1850. *Author's collection*

In the 1870s, 30 years after the 1844 report, the drains were improved and in 1875 a new sewage-pumping station (*77*) pumped sewage up St Catharine's Hill, thus alleviating problems in the city, although today sewage can still be smelled when the wind is in the east. The pumping station no longer functions and is being let as offices. Drainage was provided comparatively late at Winchester.

In 1847 the Winchester Gaslight and Coke Company was formed, later called Water and Gas Company following an act of 1865. Residual buildings from the Gas Company's premises survive between the former Corn Exchange and Moneypenny's prison on the west side of Jewry Street.

The railway to Southampton, opened in June 1839, cut off one downland slope, known as West Hill, west of the city. The isolation of this area was to trigger the relocation of various amenities. The Winchester Cemetery Company was established there by Act of Parliament in 1840 to relieve the bursting city graveyards. O.B. Carter designed the Anglican and dissenting chapels (now demolished) and the extant blue-brick gatehouse. At the same time a workhouse was created also, like the cemetery, west of and near to the railway. The prison moved to the West Hill *c.*1850 and was joined by the hospital designed by William Butterfield in 1864-8 (*78*). Police headquarters, The Diocesan Training College (1862) and the gasworks were among other public enterprises which moved there.

INSTITUTIONAL BUILDINGS

The great institutional medieval buildings, for example cathedral and Winchester College, used local flint often with ashlar brought from from a distance, for example from Caen in France or Quarr in the Isle of Wight. Some of the stone used in post-medieval Winchester was reused non-local stone from the demolished monasteries, other ecclesiastical buildings and the medieval town walls and gates: a recycling of institutional stonework. The timber framed houses at 42 (*c*.1347) and 43 (1507) High Street have later, inserted fireplaces and chimneys. At 43, described as 'le Newehouse' in 1507, the exterior of the chimney matches carving from Hyde Abbey, which a generation later probably supplied the stonework for the upgrading of this property as the old monastery was demolished (Keene 1985; James and Roberts 2000). Stonework, for example, from a demolished canon's house in The Close was documented as sent up to repair the great hall of the castle during the Civil War in 1646 (Crook 1984, 93).

Among a range of diverse building materials already appearing in the city before the railway arrived were Portland stone and Exbury yellow ('white') bricks for the Corn Exchange in (1838) in Jewry Street, by O.B. Carter (Freeman 1991). Institutional buildings, where funds were available, used new stone, for example in the churches, the Diocesan Training College (John Colson 1862) and the new guildhall (Jeffery and Skiller, 1873), which are noteworthy stone Gothic buildings of the nineteenth century.

Red brick was retained for permanent residential institutions for the middling and lower orders, decorated or not according to function and funding. Fancy diapered or patterned brickwork was employed by architects such at Garbett (St John's Hospital and Almshouses, South, 1833) and Butterfield (West Hill hospital, 1860s). A new barracks was created after 1894 when fire had almost irretrievably damaged the former palace buildings of Charles II (see *67b*). This provided an opportunity for rebuilding and the Prince of Wales laid a foundation stone in 1899 and the rainwater traps are labelled 1912 (*VCH*; Mark Allen pers. comm.). Here, echoing the palace structure, the main medium was red brick, decorated by stone details such as pillars and a pediment with coat of arms, preserved from the ruins. Although impressive to look at, the hilltop barracks was built cheaply with thin walls through which rain could be driven by the wind. With modern heating and amenities the barracks has converted well to luxury flats in recent decades. The workhouse, until recently St Paul's Hospital for the elderly and now also residential flats, is significantly lacking such architectural detail in its plain red brick, being the lowest grade institutional building. Both the mid-century prison and the workhouse were built to the cart-wheel plan, the prison with a fine central watch-tower and an impressive gateway above which hangings took place in full view of an expectant public below. The 'spokes', or wings, of these buildings could be isolated for ease of control, and the prisoners (or poor!) could be driven to the extremities to be controlled by the forces of order, reinforced from the hub.

The Winchester workhouse is a physical reminder of the changes to the poor law that occurred after the legislation of the 1830s. Built in 1834-5 it was designed to accommodate up to 300 people, drawn from Winchester and surrounding parishes.

79 The 'Cottage of the Mayor of Southampton' in 1851 on St James's Lane, facing south across the new cemetery, and known colloquially as 'The Pagoda House' gained a flash of national recognition in the *Illustrated London News* for its architectural bravado. *Author's collection*

In the event its inmates rarely exceeded 160, the number found there in 1871, and such high numbers were seasonal. Perhaps the predictions of the government about the necessity for indoor-relief were overblown. If the numbers were never excessive, the design of the building apparently proved too akin to a prison, which may account for the demolition of its exterior enclosing wall between 1871 and 1894, although its 'spoke' blocks remained (www.workhouses.org.uk for the comparative maps).

DOMESTIC AND RETAIL PREMISES

The houses of the solid middle classes pretended to be stone by employing a stuccoed effect, incised to look like blocks, as at Medecroft, Sparkford Road, 1868 (*80*), and can be seen in the private houses of Christchurch Road and further south in the St Cross area, or at the officer accommodation in St James Lane just beyond the line of the former city wall, and also along the west road beyond West Gate.

O. B. Carter was employed for a variety of domestic projects subsequent to designing the Corn Exchange, some financed by institutions such as the St John's Charity who owned many sites in the city. His designs included decorative Bath stone (harking back to the Bath stone in the city in Roman times) and yellow brick, for example at Clifton

80 Medecroft, Sparkford Road, a spacious house built in 1868 with broad vistas to the south from its veranda and upper floors. Although constrained by the high railway embankment, the very large plot, released by the Dean and Chapter, stretched from the West Hill Cemetery southwards to Airlie Road. Purchased in 1965 it now houses the University of Winchester's departments of Archaeology, History, Social Care and Tourism. *Author's collection*

Terrace which was begun during the 1840s and was still being built in 1851. At least one of Carter's designs, Chernocke Place, Southgate Street, used black porphyry for internal details, perhaps the first imports of such stone to the city since Roman times (Chris Webb, pers. comm.).

The red brick which had enjoyed such social status in the century and a half after the Civil War lost its pre-eminence to stone and stonework effects – where the stucco merely masked the bricks! – and became the material of lower-status housing in the Brooks, where the poorest people lived, and for small-scale housing in blighted areas of the suburbs around the stations and goods yards for example.

The suburbs however began to grow from the mid-nineteenth century, largely because of the enfranchisement of ecclesiastical land, formerly of the Dean and Chapter, for example along Stockbridge Road which was realigned because of the railway; at Fairfield Road (where the builder went bankrupt in the mid-1890s), near the L.S.W.R. station; at Highcliffe near the Chesil Station and to the north at Hyde where the properties were more substantial. The most numerous substantial suburban houses developed round the new Christ Church area (formerly Harold Road) in the southern suburb and further south towards St Cross, which changed its name from Sparkford. In general the quality of residential buildings improves the further they are from the stations, by contrast to the grand institutional buildings in Jewry Street *en route* to the station, and west of the railway line, for example the workhouse. The cheapness of brick no doubt led to its almost universal adoption in business premises – breweries, manufactories, workshops and stables.

ECONOMY

How did the population of Winchester earn a living? Major and continuing building works during the century provided employment for may people. The census of 1851 shows a significant number of bricklayers as heads of household and hints at social zoning. Colebrook Street, near the cathedral, chosen at random away from the suburbs, low-lying and near one of the city's streams, accommodated several households headed by bricklayers. Associated trades such as carpentry and plumbing also feature. By contrast, the second half of the century saw a decline in the number of agricultural labourers, although this trend was in part due to the reclassification of occupations within the census after 1861: over ten per cent of the male workforce was still agricultural labourers in 1871, an unusually high proportion for a town (Allen and James 2006). However, in the 1851 census, the first in which places of birth are given, the city shows a population with diverse geographical origins and varied employment.

There was industrial activity in the city such as a foundry in Colebrook Street in the 1850s, which was joined by Jewell's foundry in the Brooks from the 1870s. A number of breweries were established after 1850. These were located at the margins of the medieval walled area, such as at St Swithun Street (where the entrance, now bricked up, can be detected in the terrace near Symonds Street), St James Lane (where houses have been built over the in-filled cellars in recent years), at Eastgate Street (the former Lion Brewery, also now swept away) and the Hyde Brewery outside the site of the former north gate, and now a housing development. These locations, away from the High Street, were no doubt selected because of availability and cheapness of land. A major developer of the city suburbs in the nineteenth century was the Barrow Symonds family, whose wealth accrued from brewing into land-holding and development.

Trade directories and the census demonstrate the dominant service sector of the city's economy. In 1859 those registered in White's *Directory* bear this out: 31 bakers, 27 grocers, 27 general shopkeepers and 25 butchers, were outnumbered by 33 bricklayers, 40 booksellers and 57 insurance offices. There were 10 banks. Professionals such as lawyers (there were 22 attorneys in 1859), clergy and army officers were numerous then and are still familiar in Winchester society.

The largest group of businesses in the city in the 1859 directory was some 120 establishments providing hospitality. These ranged from hotels to inns and taverns: about a quarter of them were beerhouses. This burgeoning hospitality industry catered for local people, country people coming to market and the ever-growing numbers of visitors. Earlier in the century, Cobbett had enjoyed a market-day dinner at The Swan with farmers and 'a great number of opulent yeomen', joined after the meal by gentlemen.

RELIGION AND CULTURE

There was an air of decay about the fabric of the Anglican churches of Winchester in the early nineteenth century. At the beginning of the century there were a handful of medieval churches which, together with the fine Milner chapel of 1792 (attendance 530 on the morning of the mid-Lent census day Sunday 30 March, 200 in the evening) for Catholic worship (see *72*) and at least one private Catholic chapel, were already supplemented by nonconformist chapels. Generally, after the Emancipation Act of 1829 nonconformist places of worship became more numerous, but in Winchester, as shown below, both Catholics and varied nonconformists were well-established long before that date. The 1851 religious census demanded dates for erection of these places, and thus we see Silver Hill, Baptist (opened by John Wesley in 1785 in a private house, purchased 1817, morning 90, evening 170), Particular Baptist (before 1800, 110, 120), Independent Chapel, Congregational Dissenters (1808, 319, 200 'Congregation below the average on account of a public Immersion at the Baptist Chapel'), Wesleyan Chapel, Parchment Street (*c.*1818, 137, 134), Upper Brook Street, Wesleyan Methodist (*c.*1839, 50, 65), New Jerusalem Church, High Street (1841, attendance 14) and Chesil Street Baptist, (licensed private house in 1849 30, 35) (Vickers 1993, nos 473-94). The locations of the Catholic and nonconformist chapels are noteworthy in that they are all north of High Street, beyond the 'church and state' area south of High Street, with the exception of the suburban licensed house in Chesil Street. The Anglicans responded to resurgent Catholicism and nonconformity with Holy Trinity, north of High Street in Upper Brook Street, by Henry Woodyer (1853-4), in the Gothic reliquary style, with a flèche and a fine and very extensive series of wall-paintings emphasising High Church traditions, serving a poor parish. Apart from the chapel of the St John's almshouses, this has remained the only Anglican church north of High Street, in the town as opposed to the suburbs.

The 1851 national religious survey outlined above was the only one ever to be carried out because, it is said, the census revealed that in the country as a whole there were many more nonconformists at church on 30 March that year. The statistics were much debated. Were the returns accurate? Some places of worship, for example Winchester cathedral, sent no returns: some parish clergy refused to count their congregations. However, recorded attendance in Winchester showed over 6000 Anglicans, over 1600 nonconformists and 750 Roman Catholics from a population of 11,500 in the Winchester parishes, which included Wyke ('vulgarly Weeke' as the rector put it) and Winnall. Thus Anglicans with over 70 per cent of all the churchgoers in the Winchester census far outstripped their competitors, as might be predicted in a cathedral city, and went strongly against the national trend. In defending themselves against charges of national preponderance of Nonconformists, Anglicans argued that whereas they attended church on average once on Sunday, Nonconformists went twice, thus accounting for their larger numbers. If this was the case in Winchester the Anglicans were even more overwhelming numerically. There was, incidentally, at that time no synagogue and no church of the Latter Day Saints. But Mormonism was not unknown in Winchester in 1851 as we find a native of Guernsey and an 'elder' (aged 22) of the Latter Day Saints as a visitor among the poor, in the variously-spelt 'Poulsome' Place, Middle Brook Street (Mark Allen, pers. comm.).

Church attendance by all denominations was thus over 70 per cent, 3 per cent above the county average. There are no returns for certain sizeable parishes such as St Peter

81 St Maurice Church in the High Street, rebuilt in 1842 to Gothic designs by the architect Gover, it retained some ancient Romanesque features which can now be seen in the residual tower. The rest of the building made way for Sheriff and Ward, now Debenhams, *c.*1960 (WCM PWCM 4440)

Colebrook, which had a population of 604, and St Faith with a population of 892, although people from these parishes attended elsewhere, as there were by 1851 no extant churches with those dedications, casualties of the decline from some 57 to fewer than a dozen between 1148 and 1600. The extent to which individuals attended more than once when many places of worship recorded three services cannot be known (Vickers 1993).

The growing population of the city from 1801 to 1851 was matched by a rise in church attendance. The fine nineteenth-century ecclesiastical buildings surviving in the city bear witness to the enthusiasm of the faithful to provide sufficient and up-to-date accommodation for their diverse spiritual needs. As the century progressed, the medieval churches of the city and suburbs were renovated, such as the derelict church of St Bartholomew, Hyde, or rebuilt, such as St Maurice in the High Street (Gover, 1842) (*81*) and St Martin, Winnall (Coles, 1858). Old St Thomas, which gave its name to the street where it had stood for centuries, was demolished in 1845 amid vociferous protests from conservationists. New St Thomas west of Southgate Street was complete in 1846, and was consecrated in April 1847, with a tower finished in 1857. It was considered by the authoritative architectural analyst Nikolaus Pevsner (1967) to be the best Gothic Revival church in the city. The spacious St Thomas was supplemented by additional Anglican places of worship after 1850: Holy Trinity, already mentioned, Christ Church (1858), St Paul, Weeke (1873) and finally All Saints, Highcliffe (1890-8). By this time the church-building movement was in decline and the bell-tower of All Saints was never completed (Pevsner and Lloyd 1967). These churches and chapels were built and decorated largely in stone, which ranged from flint with ashlar quoins, window reveals and decorations at Holy Trinity in the poor Brooks, to fine ashlar work at Christ Church in the wealthy and growing southern suburb.

Winchester's associations with Jane Austen, who died in the city in 1817 (*82*), and with John Keats who was inspired by the water meadows to write his poem 'To Autumn', the season of 'mellow fruitfulness', on visiting Winchester in 1819, are well known. Later in the century Anthony Trollope in his novel *The Warden* (1855), dwelt on the St Cross scandal in which the Reverend Francis North, fifth Earl of Guilford, was found in 1808 to have derived more than £300,000 from his corrupt tenure of the office of Master of St Cross Hospital. That he was appointed by his father, Brownlow North (bishop 1781-1820), who had himself been appointed to Winchester by his brother the Prime Minister, made the scandal worse. Francis North, one of a number of family friends appointed by Brownlow North, also improperly held a canonry at the cathedral and two other livings in the diocese.

The fabric of the cathedral in the first part of the century (*colour plate 14* and cover) was indeed in a poor state of repair and the acerbic William Cobbett, while he may not have been representative of general attitudes no doubt spoke for many. After visiting a Sunday service at the cathedral in 1830 he wrote:

> There is a dean, and God knows how many prebends belong to this immensely rich bishopric and its chapter: and there were at this service, two or three men and five or six boys in white surplices, with a congregation of fifteen women and four men! Gracious God!

With such a start to the century in ecclesiastical affairs, matters could only improve. The appointment of the evangelical and youthful Charles Sumner as bishop in 1827 led to many changes. The chapter of the cathedral was reformed, and the training of teachers for the diocese was instituted with the foundation of the Training College in 1840. The bishop's daughter-in-law, Mary Sumner, founded the Mothers' Union which grew by her death to have hundreds of thousands of members, while other women's organisations also grew from the city led by a cohort of dedicated Anglican women based in the city in the closing decades of the nineteenth century.

The great ecclesiastical buildings and the obvious antiquity of Winchester attracted numerous artists and subsequently photographers. Samuel Prout's view of Middle Brook Street (1813) has already been mentioned. G.F. Prosser (1805-82) lived in Winchester from 1852 and died in St John's Almshouses. He had published *Select Illustrations of Winchester* in 1833. Among his better-known views is the cathedral cemetery, full of leaning tombstones (1849), before the stones were removed and the ground lowered after 1882. Beatrice Corfe (*c.*1866-1947 – she was aged five in the census of 1871, and 80 when she died), who lived in Chesil Street, was commissioned by the architect, builder and mayor, Thomas Stopher to paint views of Winchester at the turn of the century. Among her work is a watercolour of the Old Pleasure Fair in the Broadway (1897) and remarkable interiors such as that, now in the possession of the Victoria and Albert

82 The house where Jane Austen died in 1817, in College Street next to Winchester College's Headmaster's House by G.S. Repton (1839-42). *Photograph John Crook*

Museum, of the wealthy Canon Valpy's beautifully furnished drawing room at *c.*1900 at 3 The Close, now The Pilgrims' School (James 1993 nos.87, 88).

Canon Valpy's house in The Close and those of the other senior clergy of the diocese would have been familiar to Charlotte Mary Yonge (1823-1901) whose novels use the ecclesiastical scene at Winchester for a setting. Similarly, she would have known of The Black Swan hotel 'an inn of repute on the High Street, and at no distance from the station' where, after a two hour train journey from London Sherlock Holmes and Dr Watson met Miss Hunter in Conan Doyle's dramatic story *The Copper Beeches* (1892).

Tourism grew during the century: among various reasons why Winchester grew were that people found it congenial, and encouraged others to follow. Its antiquities attracted visitors such as Cobbett. From soon after its foundation in 1885 the Hampshire Field Club was encouraging members, some of whom became very expert on the city, to meet near the railway station for expeditions. The visitor trade burgeoned so that by 1900 there was a broad range of souvenirs being offered to tourists, such as Goss china souvenirs which began to appear from 1880 showing Winchester heraldry and icons. However English varieties, such as Goss made at Hanley, Stoke-on-Trent, in the Midland potteries, and local souvenir ceramics, were being challenged by cheap imports such as teapots and other china 'garish in colour and fussy in design' made in Germany,

83 Like Jane Austen, who died in 1819, Charlotte Yonge (1823-1901), devotee of John Keble the Anglican reforming vicar of Hursley who had died in 1866, was a local author who was afforded a commemorative niche in the Cathedral. This historic photograph shows the reredos in the north transept chapel. *Author's collection*

some inscribed in appropriate Gothic script 'A Present from Winchester' (WMNS 28, 29 1997). Winchester's Saxon past, the great enthusiasm for Germany, whence England drew its royalty, made Winchester with its Germanic past a focus. The belief that the Germanic Saxons had exterminated the British/Welsh 'gibberish' speakers was very popular. John Richard Green's astonishingly popular *Short History of the English People* (1874), hailed England as the 'only purely German nation which rose upon the wreck of Rome' (James 2003, 44). Germans, united since 1871, saw the Saxon conquest of England as an early example of Germanic empire-building, empire building taken by descendants of those Germans to the four corners of the globe by their British cousins. The Alfred millenary celebrations which coincided with the year of Queen Victoria's death in 1901 were a facet of this enthusiasm (Yorke 1999). How different attitudes to Germany were to become a generation later and to remain until the end of the millennium.

EDUCATION

Beatrice Corfe became an art teacher, and the censuses show numbers of art and music teachers as well as other school staff. The census convention for describing the majority of children as 'scholars' suggests an awareness of the growing importance of education – even if such appellations do not mean that the children were studying. From the Forster Education Act of 1870 School Boards were allowed to pay for schools on the rates if provision at the elementary level was insufficient.

Winchester College, which had languished in the eighteenth century, began to revive in the nineteenth. Especially under Headmaster George Ridding, who handed over to Dr Fearon in 1884, the college made great progress in modernisation. Facilities such as the development of the houses spread across the southern part of the city, as seen in the 1871 census, above, and the fine gymnasium (1875-80) hint at 'muscular Christianity' which was such a feature of the second half of the nineteenth century. By 1875 Winchester, owners of the original cricket ground at Broadhalfpenny Down, Hambledon, had already played Eton at cricket for nigh on half a century.

Education became more broadly based in the nineteenth century. The foundation of many parish and denominational schools, of which St Faith's is among surviving schools today, spread education down the social scale. Education for girls was provided by St Swithun's School at 17 Southgate Street when it opened in 1884, and subsequently at North Walls where it remained until 1930. Peter Symonds College opened in 1897 as a school for boys aged 11-18 at 39 Southgate Street and moved to Owen's Road by 1899. In addition, a number of preparatory schools were founded in the late nineteenth century such as Westfield, later called West Downs, which occupied buildings created *c.*1880 by the philanthropic Lord Northbrook for the Winchester Modern School, and set in generous playing fields. The school and playing fields have recently returned to public educational use as teaching and student accommodation of the University of Winchester, with its former Masters' Lodge, where the masters lived, added in good arts and crafts style in 1905, now a centre for postgraduate research.

The nineteenth century saw a transformation from a sleepy country town of some 6000 souls to a city of some 20,000 people, with a varied economy and society. A microcosm of the spirit of the age was that Charles Benny, a grocer, hotelier and Conservative politician, led the Winchester Cemetery Company, which in 1840 took over burial rights that the church had monopolised in the city since Saxon times. As the nineteenth century gave way to the twentieth, Winchester was thriving demographically, economically and socially, with flourishing religious groups and with a broadening educational base.

10

MODERN WINCHESTER: FROM 1900

The twentieth century was dominated by two world wars, and for Britain by withdrawal from Empire. To the west of the cathedral, where the Roman Forum and early Saxon royal palace once stood, there are two substantial war memorials. At Winchester College there is the peaceful war cloister to commemorate the 500 Wykehamists (virtually none Winchester *oppidans*) who 'were found faithful even unto death'; at the University of Winchester the Winton memorial chapel records over 80 names of men who died; 116 War Graves Commission graves are found in the West Hill Cemetery, together with graves of six Germans who died during internment. All these memorials were enlarged with the casualties from the Second World War.

The Winchester Roll of Honour compiled after the Great War by A. Cecil Piper recorded 3454 servicemen from the city, 459 of whom died in the course of the war. Their remains are scattered, a few in India, Iran and Turkey, some seamen, many in Iraq, most along the Western Front, a few in the West Hill Cemetery in Winchester itself. Their records tell microcosmically the terrible tale of war: death in action, accidental death, missing believed killed, drownings, wounds and sickness. The deliberations of the war memorial committee ranged widely from a grand 'Temple of Honour' on St Giles Hill, or a memorial thoroughfare from the West End of the cathedral to Southgate Street, to a 'Victory Arch and Gateway' to the cathedral from Market Street (rejected as 'most unsuitable' … 'from an artistic point of view'), to utilitarian schemes such as 'baths and canteens for the children of the poor', opposed as potentially unmemorable and as the inspiration of 'the materialistic attitudes of the puritan forces in our midst' (Atkins 1999). The memorial records that Hampshire people gave their lives in a tradition of 'service and sacrifice handed down from King Alfred', a legacy no doubt in the minds of those who took the decision to change the name of The Diocesan training College to King Alfred's College a few years later, in 1928.

The military focus of the city has declined steadily through the twentieth century: the Russian gun from the Crimean War, the centre of a riot over proposals to remove it

84 In 1979 to celebrate the 900th anniversary of the foundation on the cathedral, the author organised a historic procession of characters from Winchester's history from early Christian times to the twentieth century, closing with William Walker the diver and George Mallory who scaled Everest. Here we see part of the procession gathering in The Close – Aethelwold, Canute (adjusting his crown), Queen Emma, with King William Rufus, a medieval bishop and Sir Walter Raleigh among others in the background. *Photograph A. V. Lee*

from the High Street in 1908, was quietly scrapped to supply the needs of the Second World War. A Boer gun from the South African War and a tank donated in return for the generous support from Winchester people who purchased war bonds during the First World War have disappeared, probably in the same cause. There is now no sign of the gun on St Giles Hill for which £50, to match that for compilation of the Roll of Honour, was voted by the War Memorial Committee in 1919. The barracks, which incorporated the site of Roman structures and the medieval castle, has been sold for exclusive residential purposes. Residual military museums in that sector of the city stand as monuments to the past. A new barracks outside the city, at Flowerdown, has less impact on Winchester.

Winchester remains a centre of local government. At least one whole street, Westgate Lane, was demolished for the building of the Hampshire County Council Buildings, and where there are current plans for another major development programme. Local government reorganisation in 1974 brought the ancient boroughs of Southampton and Portsmouth under Hampshire County Council, though in 1997 these great cities once more became unitary authorities, significantly reducing the authority of the

85 The Hampshire Record Office, Sussex Street, the brain-child of Councillor Freddie Emery-Wallis supported by Hampshire County Council, was designed by Colin Stansfield-Smith and was opened by the Queen and the Duke of Edinburgh on 19 November 1993. It houses the records of Hampshire and the Bishopric of Winchester, and is only one of two county record offices in the country whose collections are designated as of both national and international importance. *Photograph John Crook*

HCC, which has slid down the table of wealthy local authorities as a result, and the administrative impact of Winchester concomitantly declined. The surviving railway station announces Winchester as the home of Hampshire County Council. The city 'district' council has built new offices near the Guildhall and the cathedral, with a Museum Service, supporting the City Museum in The Square, at 75 Hyde Street and with stores at Bar End. The County Museum Service stores are found also at Bar End, now with a fine new focus at the Milestones Museum at Basingstoke. Undoubtedly the outstanding building of recent years is the Hampshire Record Office, near the station, where the records of this most ancient city and its county are preserved in purpose-built accommodation (*85*). This, together with the extensive programme of archaeology, which has been a theme of this book, epitomises current interest in the past of England in a post-imperial age. Links with Europe have strengthened economically, socially and with tourism, reflecting much of the city's medieval European heritage, when pilgrims were the tourists, and the visitor can hardly fail to notice that Winchester's past and present were shaped by Romans, Saxons and Normans.

BEFORE 1918

In 1901 the city enjoyed anniversary celebrations for the millennium of the death of King Alfred (died 899), which should properly have been celebrated in 1899. However, the indefatigable mayor Alfred Bowker throwing chronological rectitude to the four winds, masterminded activities which culminated, so far as Alfred the Great was concerned, with the erection of Hamo Thornycroft's 'heroic peasant' statue in the Broadway, and so far as Bowker was concerned, with the issue of a commemorative medal with his own visage on one side and King Alfred's on the other! Academics, in the know about the dates, were allowed to process in their scholarly finery, but not to interfere with the splendid festivities organised by the mayor, over details such as the date of Alfred's death (Yorke 1999).

The city appears a comfortable place in the Edwardian period. The many postcards of that era have views of bustling streets and sleepy suburbs. Trade directories show the arrival of multiple stores such as the Maypole Dairy, Boots the Chemist and the International Stores. These new enterprises were strongly capitalised and had an impact on ancient buildings in the city. Boots bought the Gudgeon arcade in The Pentice for £4000 in 1903, demolished it and rebuilt in mock-medieval timbering adorned with carvings of bishops, on the site. International Stores chopped a building of c.1460 out of The Pentice, threatening Thomas Stopher, the architect, another active Winchester one-time mayor, who protested, that if he refused to provide a plan for a new structure (with more floor space, as at Boots), he would be summarily sacked and a more compliant professional appointed. Stopher's rectangular façade in London brick stands to this day amidst the steep roofs of its surviving medieval neighbours.

Increasing demands of traffic began to take a toll and led to the demolition of buildings for road-widening, a notable early example being the corner of Chesil Street and Morn Hill, north of Chesil Rectory.

A threat to the cathedral from subsidence occurred early in the century. The great church was preserved by the strenuous efforts of William Walker, a diver who worked under the supervision of architects Colson and Jackson on the permanently flooded foundations to replace with concrete a medieval wooden 'raft' on which the cathedral was originally built. A significant change to the southern aspect of the cathedral resulted from the erection of (individually-sponsored) buttresses, which encroached on the area of the pre-Reformation cloister (Henderson and Crook, 1994).

King George V visited Winchester on St Swithun's Day 1912 on the occasion of a service in celebration of the completion of the cathedral repairs. A commemorative card stated that this was the first official visit by a reigning monarch since Queen Anne – nearly two centuries before. Winchester had proved a suitable venue for a major international gathering of military attachés in 1910, based at the George Hotel. The Great War brought many soldiers to the city for training and in transit. Prisoners of War were detained on Winnall Down at the site of the long-vanished medieval leper hospital.

DEMOGRAPHIC CHANGE

In the course of the twentieth century the city has continued to grow in size from over 20,000 in 1900 to over 30,000 by 1971, a figure which has recently risen once more. The rise has not by any means been regular during the century. By 1911 it was 23,378 and was 403 higher in 1921; in 1931 down to 22,970. There was no census in 1941 but by 1951 the figure had risen to 25,721, although this reflects boundary changes in 1932–5. The population continued to rise steadily: 28,770 in 1961 and 31,107 in 1971. Boundary changes in the 1970s led to a decline to 29,337 in 1981. In 1991 the population had crept up again to 29,758 since when it had risen to 34,736 in 2001, with a projection of 35,523 at the time of writing in 2006 (www.hants.gov.uk/factsand figures).

A major reason for this recent growth has been the development of the former Diocesan Training College (1840, moved to the current site in 1862 for 56 students) which became King Alfred's College (1928), University College Winchester (2004) and the University of Winchester in 2005. In 1958 the decision was taken to admit women and to increase numbers to make a college of 250 men and 150 women. By the 150th anniversary in 1990 there were 1500 full-time students and many part-timers. Today there are some 5500 students at the University studying a broad range of topics from Archaeology and Business to Creative Writing, Drama, Film, Education, History, Music, Performing Arts, Psychology, Theology and Religious Studies, Sports Studies and much else. Students work at undergraduate and postgraduate level and come from around the globe. Much of the research since 1996 into Winchester's past has been achieved through doctoral studies of the city, locality and region and the university is also making its name in a broad range of research areas, many with an international dimension. Winchester University is the only university in Hampshire, and receives strong support from the Hampshire County Council. The Lord-Lieutenant of Hampshire is the first Chancellor of the University, and the Vice-Chancellor is also a woman, so great have been the changes since the 1950s. Analysis of the 2001 census for the Winchester District revealed that Winchester had the highest proportion of migrants in Hampshire, at 15 per cent, attributed to the presence during term time of students (www.hants.gov/census; James and Doughty 1991).

SOCIAL CONDITIONS BETWEEN THE WARS

Following the Great War improved residential accommodation began to be provided for poorer people whose families had been so mutilated by the war. In 1919 the city council Housing Committee declared that Winchester was almost entirely a residential area.

Winchester in the 1920s, although crowded in comparison with its past history, was not crowded by twentieth-century urban standards elsewhere. Persons per acre in Winchester were computed as 12.3 for the 1921 census, compared with 17.5 at Southampton and 31 at Portsmouth. The response to the need for working-class housing was the outstanding Stanmore estate, homes truly fit for returning heroes to live in. The houses at Stanmore were provided with parlours, but only after a national debate which was fuelled by fears that talking might lead to insurrection! Plans of Stanmore were displayed at the Wembley Exhibition of 1922 as a model estate. Female employment in the city was comparatively high at 33 per cent of the work-force in 1921, one element in this being the remarkable figure of 68 per 1000 women who were in personal service. This employment structure corresponded to the social and economic make-up of the city, with army, clergy, lawyers and the medical profession well represented.

The 1926 General Strike affected Winchester, where a small Labour movement confronted the Conservative authorities and where, by contrast some students from the Training College went to Southampton docks to unload ships during the nine-day stoppage.

Housing spread westwards from Stanmore Lane towards Battery Hill while, to the south-east of the city, 300 houses were added to Highcliffe in 1926-7. The changing population of this comparatively affluent city was catered for by an increasing number of multiple stores which proliferated between the wars, including Woolworth's (1929) and Marks and Spencer (1935), both of which developed sites on the north side of the High Street.

The steady development in building of the 1920s, as exemplified in the Catholic church of St Peter (completed 1928) and the new St Swithun's School for girls (completed 1930), reflected a liberalisation of attitudes to Catholics (the Italians were on the allied side in the Great War) and to women who had contributed so much to the war effort, and who finally achieved equal voting rights with men in 1928. The 1920s were comparatively prosperous and hopeful.

But the crash of 1929 hit institutional as well as individual fortunes. The Church suffered financially and lay institutional building virtually dried up in the city in 1932 when some council buildings outside West Gate to the south were completed. It is significant in this respect that although designs for the great County Hall to the north of West Gate were prepared in the 1930s by Cowles-Voysey, it was not built until 1959-60. The major building work of the 1930s was the bypass (*86*), a small echo of continental road building at that time, and perhaps built with some of the same purposes as the more extensive works in Germany – to provide employment after the depression, and with an eye to the return of war to Europe. By carrying military traffic round the city it may have served the twin functions of saving Winchester from destruction of buildings to facilitate movement of equipment, and also from bombing which afflicted so many centres of communication.

THE SECOND WORLD WAR TO THE PRESENT

One bomb fell at Hyde, killing people and damaging property. Recently rediscovered air raid shelters beneath the car-park behind the City Library (Corn Exchange) in Jewry Street, contain patriotic graffiti including cartoons of Hitler and Mussolini, as well as drawings representative of the wartime pre-occupations of those who took refuge there – soldiers, ships and planes, all scrawled on the walls. After the Second World War,

86 Winchester bypass was built in the 1930s to relieve the traffic bottleneck at Winchester. It was then one of only a handful of dual carriageways in the country, echoing the great motorways of Italy and Germany, and was therefore dubbed 'one of Britain's most modern roads'. *Kate Brooker/author*

austerity bit deep and the city fell into disrepair until, with returning prosperity in the mid-1950s, building began again. The demands of the motor car became increasingly felt: street widening brought about the destruction of the commodious George Hotel (the site now partly under the road and partly occupied by Barclays Bank) on the High Street in 1956 and the closure of the West Gate to traffic in the 1960s. In 1958 a science block and New Hall at Winchester College were created, the latter describe by Nikolaus Pevsner as 'a curious and in many ways regrettable building' (1967, 706), with the County Council building, named Queen Elizabeth Court, completed in 1959-60.

These developments were followed by a spate of building throughout the city: for example the Wessex Hotel in 1961-2, adjacent to the cathedral, which was one of the sites made available to archaeologists, funded by the new prosperity (*6*). A key change which affected residents from the 1960s onwards was the institution of an electric railway service to London. Thenceforward there has been a service which reaches the capital before 9a.m.: this enabled daily commuting for workers rather than directors and transformed employment opportunities for residents, and compares well with Conan Doyle's two hour train-journey from London (Utrick Casebourne, pers. comm.).

Since then, building and development have become part of the life of the city: commercial premises in the city centre; an industrial estate at Winnall; major additions to housing stock took place at Badger Farm, Harestock, Oliver's Battery, Teg Down, Weeke and Winnall. The Brooks Centre completed in 1991 was the major development of the 1990s (*87*), and pays homage to the city's Roman Heritage in its massive scale and some detail of its decoration, but has been much criticised for its eclectic style and

87 The Brooks Centre, a controversial major shopping development completed on the site of former nineteenth-century housing where post-medieval gardens, medieval, Saxon and Roman housing has previously existed. Among debates at the time the inclusion of underground parking was significant because of its damage to the archaeological record. *Photograph John Crook*

its inhospitable, wind-swept interior. Across the road, west of the Brooks Centre, there are current plans for very large developments between Middle Brook Street, Tanner Street (Lower Brook Street) and Friarsgate, an area previously developed in the 1960s. The plans also include building on the long-established site of the Bus Station, carrying development through from Silver Hill to High Street.

Beyond the former walled area increased capacity and replacement of buildings has taken place at the hospital, the new buildings capitalising on spectacular views southwards down the Itchen Valley. Clearance of sites for these works has been the spur for renewed excavation of early Winchester, described above. The development and expansion of the University has also contributed significant building and refurbishment programmes to the architecture of the city. The adaption of the original buildings at West Downs campus has already been referred to, to which may be added the building of award-winning 'green' student accommodation on the former playing fields there. The rebuilt (John) Stripe Theatre at the King Alfred's campus is now being dwarfed by the creation of the new University Centre, partly dug into the chalk hillside, and echoing on a grand scale the 'collapsed tent' architecture as Pevsner described it, of the former Dining Hall, a casualty of the new development (Pevsner and Lloyd, 1967; *colour plates 22* and *23*).

At the end of the 1980s Winchester was dubbed the wealthiest city in Britain: a packed station car-park each morning bore witness to the exodus to work in London at that time.

The early 1990s were less certain, but the new millennium has brought renewed vigour to the links with London, and property prices in the city have continued to rise. Many gardens have been built over; in suburban streets such as Chilbolton Avenue, in addition, family houses have made way for multi-occupation dwellings. Elsewhere the city boasts houses being marketed for comfortably over £1 million and new flats starting at £500,000.

Winchester became synonymous with the long battle to save Twyford Down from destruction in a new bypass project (*colour plate 21*). Although the Down was not ultimately saved, the campaign contributed to a temporary reconsideration of government transport policy on road-building, sustaining Winchester's place on the national stage. Much information swirled around the Twyford Down road cutting. Some said there was an error in computing the length (and therefore the cost) of a tunnel, because a direct tunnel would have been shorter than the sinuous road cutting, but that point was overlooked. Others claimed that a tunnel was ruled out on security grounds because of ease of movement of large-scale American military equipment from a base on the Solent. Such were the heady conspiracy theories at that contested time. It is no coincidence that throughout its existence the city has been a focus for routes, for the majority of the period its masters seeking to exploit the position on the north–south route in the Itchen valley and the east–west route along the downs, but in recent years Winchester city governors have sought to keep the fumes and noise of modern transport at bay.

THE FUTURE OF WINCHESTER'S PAST

Key matters remain for investigation by present and future archaeologists of Winchester. They can be highlighted by period. The pre-Iron Age needs further examination. For the Iron Age, the relationship between St Catharine's Hill, the Oram's Arbour site and the surrounding countryside need exploration. The end of the Iron Age and the coming of the Romans need elucidation. Was there a clean break or continuity of settlement? Was the market of the Belgae (Venta Belgarum) a folk-memory or a going concern after the invasion in AD 43? What are the connections between the villa culture of the hinterland and the early Roman city, and subsequently?

The earliest Roman activities remain mysterious. Was there a fort and if so where? What was the sequence of the earliest Roman settlements in the city? From the Roman period, key monuments remain undiscovered, unrecognised and unexcavated; the basilica in the forum, the Roman theatre and Roman baths (although a potential fragment of a bath-structure was found on the eastern city wall in 1988, WMSN 26, 1996) are examples. There is a lack of information on Roman religion, for example on temples in Venta. There is also much to be learnt about the end of Roman Winchester. To what extent did Roman remains, other than the earthworks of the walls, remain upstanding in the post-Roman period?

For the Saxon period the issues begin with the question of continuity, or lack of it from the Roman past. There appears to be a cessation in activity within the walled area in the early fifth century. Do the cemeteries of Roman date and post-Roman date which contain, for example, decapitated bodies, indicate a continuity of anything other than violence? Can we now dispense with invasion theories for both Romans and Saxons, and be satisfied with long-term settlement patterns as a replacement? If there was continuity, what was its nature, and who were the power-brokers? Were they resurgent British, or immigrant warriors? What is the relationship between the cemeteries around the city and Winchester itself in the early Saxon period and were there early churches adjacent to early Christian burials, for example in the later seventh century?

In later Saxon Winchester there are gaps, for example an increasing amount is known about Viking and Scandinavian influences on the city but artefactual evidence is at present scarce. Were the Vikings the fierce invaders of the kind sent to be hanged by Alfred in 896, or were they merely refugees driven from their northern outposts by climate change and overpopulation? Saxon domestic housing awaits further analysis and interpretation. None the less, broadly speaking, the development of Saxon England can be charted through the archaeology of the city and its hinterland.

We now know much about medieval Winchester, but await, for example, a definitive pottery sequence. Certain major sites such as the royal palace and Magdalen leper hospital remain to be investigated. From the eleventh century onwards increasing survival of documentation facilitates quantification, and analysis by occupation and status of population and society. The contribution of below-ground archaeology and the study of standing remains together with documentary evidence combine to give, for Winchester, an especially detailed and integrated account of social archaeology and social history.

Post-Reformation Winchester is comparatively less well studied, but none the less much has been achieved over the last 40 years or so beginning with Tom Atkinson's *Elizabethan Winchester* (1963), which was followed by Adrienne Rosen's doctoral thesis on the society and economy of the city in the sixteenth and seventeenth centuries (1975). Nikolaus Pevsner's and David Lloyd's *Hampshire* (1967) in the Buildings of England series, although now somewhat outdated on the medieval city, made an especially important contribution in listing many post-medieval buildings. He grouped by period, from their exteriors, the great red brick houses from the period of the Restoration and eighteenth century and offered dates for certain of them. In the last decade examination and analysis of post-medieval sources under the auspices of The Winchester Project has cast much new light on citizens and city government, on Winchester houses, their owners and contents, supplemented by smaller studies such as that of the war memorials and Roll of Honour after the First World War and by local publications such as the Hampshire Papers and *Hampshire Studies*.

The city has enjoyed a period of extensive excavation since the Second World War. Information from these excavations is slowly coming to light through publication and through exhibitions and lectures. The bulk of the excavations remain to be published, which makes this account interim in nature. However, the major monuments continue to attract visitors to the ancient capital of England as they have done for a thousand years and more. A walk through the city reveals a treasure-house of architecture of all periods set in riverine parks and a glorious chalkland landscape.

GLOSSARY

Antonine(s)	Roman emperors from Antoninus Pius to Commodus, AD 138-92
Atrebates	A tribe who settled in pre-Roman southern England
bishopric pipe roll	The annual account and manorial roll for the estates of the bishops of Winchester
Brooks, The	North-eastern quarter of the city, so called because of the brooks or water-courses, now covered over, which run down upper, middle and Lower Brook Street (Tanner Street). The Brooks excavations (1987-8) investigated an area between Middle and Upper Brook Street
burh	An Anglo-Saxon defended settlement
chi-rho	First two letter of Christ's name, a Christian symbol
Close, The	Area surrounding the cathedral. To the south and east is the Inner Close where the post-Conquest priory stood. This area is still closed at night. To the north and west is the Outer Close, no longer enclosed, where the Old and New Minsters stood
dendrochronology	The science of dating timber by analysis of tree-rings to give a date when timber was felled, often coterminous with first use when timber was used green
Flavian(s)	Roman emperors from Vespasian to Domitian, AD 69-96
gild merchant	Originally a body of merchants which in the Middle Ages became synonymous with town government (and which included non-merchants)
hide	A measure of land notionally 49ha (120 acres)
Hospital of St John	A charitable foundation of which some medieval buildings survive north of The Broadway. Substantial additional buildings were added south of the The Broadway in 1833. Series of almshouses are found at both locations

illumination	The embellishment of a manuscript with colour
insula	A rectangular area within a notional grid laid over a plan of the city identified by number beginning with Roma I at the forum and working outwards towards the walls
long-and-short work	A characteristic of Saxon stone building technique in which corners were reinforced by stones laid with the long sides alternately upright and horizontal
machicolations	Openings in military architecture between corbels supporting a parapet, through which missiles could be thrown on attackers
PPG 16	Planning Policy Guidance. Department of the Environment planning advice which addresses the integration of archaeology into the planning process
Purbeck marble	A shelly limestone (and therefore not a true marble) usually from Dorset which takes a high polish
Samian ware	A fine-fabric pottery of first to third century AD, usually red with decoration
Soke, The	Areas of the southern and eastern suburbs under the jurisdiction of the bishop, from 'soke', i.e. a local jurisdiction. Also the name of a large house in Chesil Street
spolia	Statuary etc. taken from ancient civilisations and used to decorate medieval buildings
staple	A principal market or measuring place for a particular commodity, for example, wool, as in Staple Gardens
tarrage	From the French, *terre,* i.e. a land tax
tesserae	Small square/cuboid pieces used to make mosaic pavements
tufa	Porous calcareous stone
visitation returns	Answers by clergy to standard sets of questions issued by bishops as 'visitors' of parishes
Wolvesey	Originally Wulf's Isle, an area within the south-eastern quarter of the city walls, long occupied by the bishop's residence

A TOUR OF THE CITY

(Numbers in bold refer to the map on p.174)

Begin at the Tourist Information Centre in the Guildhall (**1**), the Broadway (see *88*).

Leaflets are available and monument opening times can be checked. Tours are available with qualified guides twice daily Easter to October, Saturday mornings in the winter.

Thereafter start with the cathedral. Apart from the building itself visit the Triforium Gallery and the cathedral library to see in particular the Winchester Bible. Outside the cathedral to the north look at the display which shows the development of Old Minster (**2**; see *22*). To the south note the remains of the monastic buildings (see *62*), the Deanery (medieval prior's lodging), the 'Pilgrims' Hall' with its timber roof of *c.*1310 and the fifteenth-century stables by the gate (**3**). Passing out of the Prior's Gate (**4**), the adjacent King's Gate with its little church over it is of interest.

Left under the gate along College Street takes you past the house (**5**) where Jane Austen died (see *82*) to Winchester College (**6**) (10.00-13.00, 14.00-17.00; tours April-September) with its fourteenth-century Chamber Court, chapel and the remarkable statue of the Virgin Mary over the Outer Gate. Beyond the college on the left is Wolvesey Palace (**7**) rebuilt incorporating the medieval chapel in the late seventeenth-century. This is the home of the bishop. Beside it are the remains of medieval Wolvesey. Beyond Wolvesey follow the high wall round The Weirs gardens beside the river, re-routed here by the Romans, a fragment of whose wall can be seen preserved towards the City Bridge end of the gardens (**8**).

At the City Bridge visit the City Mill (**9**; April-September 11.00-16.45, March and October, Saturday and Sunday 12.00-16.00, National Trust) and pass into the High Street by way of St John's Almshouses, South (**10**; see *76*), which have '1833' in the east gable. Across the road are the north almshouses with their hall and chapel. The Thornycroft statue of King Alfred (**11,** see *20*) dominates the High Street and has the Abbey gardens beside it (**12**). This was the site of the medieval Nunnaminster (see *61*) where part of the

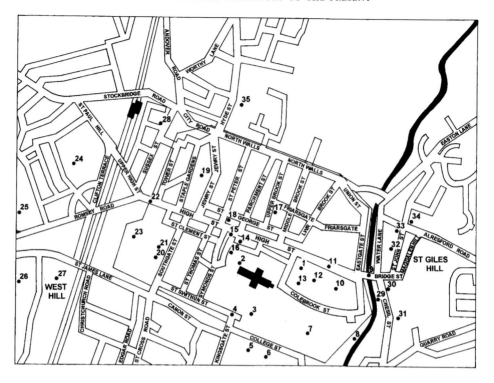

88 Map showing sites and monuments referred to in the tour outlined here

structure can be seen displayed immediately west of the Guildhall. Abbey House, now the mayor's offices, is in the gardens and also the Abbey Mill with its fine portico (**13**).

In the High Street, nos. 33 and 34 (see *48*) are intact medieval structures under The Pentice (**14**). The Buttercross (see *52*) and the adjacent penticed 42 High Street are medieval (**15**). Behind 41 and 42 High Street is St Lawrence church and the City Museum (**16***; April–September, Monday–Friday 10.00–17.00, Saturday 10.00–13.00, 14.00–17.00, closed on Mondays October–March) is nearby adjacent to The Close at the west end of the cathedral where the Visitor Centre offers refreshments and a shop. Allow over two hours for a guided tour such as this, which would include 20 minutes in the cathedral (but not, for example, the Triforium Gallery and the cathedral library). Individuals would cover the ground more quickly, and could take in the West Gate and great hall (below) within two hours.

Up the High Street towards the West gate, Godbegot House (**18**) on the north side is a fine timber-framed courtyard house with the site of the medieval church of St Peter marked out on the paving behind beside St George Street. Jewry Street, to the north of the High Street, contains the former County Gaol (1805); Corn Exchange (**19***; 1838, O.B. Carter, now City Library) and the Theatre Royal. To the south of the High Street, Southgate Street has several fine eighteenth-century buildings, including Serle's House, now the Hampshire Regiment Museum (**20**), also on the west side St Thomas church, arguably the best Gothic Revival church in Winchester (**21**).

The medieval West Gate (**22**; includes museum open as City Museum but closed November-January inclusive) is at the top of the High Street. Adjacent on raised ground are ruins of a rounded tower and sally port of the castle, and the unrivalled thirteenth-century great hall (**23**; see *41*) (April-October 10.00-17.00, November-March 10.00-16.00). Behind the hall is a small reconstructed medieval garden. Beyond the castle hall are remains of Charles II's palace built into the Peninsula Barracks, an impressive brick structure of the 1890s, beside which are found further military museums (Royal Hussars, Light Infantry, Brigade of Gurkhas, Royal Green Jackets), entered from the medieval garden. From here it is an easy stroll back to the Guildhall in the Broadway where the tour began.

THE SUBURBS

West

The western suburb contains the area of Oram's Arbour where major Iron Age discoveries have been made (**24**; see *12*). It is flanked to the west by the remains of a large twelfth-century bank, which marks the limit of an incomplete circuit of the city defences. Otherwise the suburb contains a fine collection of nineteenth-century institutional structures: hospital, prison (**25**), training college (**26**), and cemetery with gatehouse (**27**), and also some fine terraced and detached residences. At its junction with the northern suburb are found the railway station and the Hampshire Record Office (**28**; see *85*).

South

St Catharine's Hill and Twyford Down (now in part a stretch of the M3) are both significant prehistoric sites which lie to the south of the city. St Catharine's Hill (see *11*) is topped by a maze marked on the ground. Also to the south of the city lies the village of St Cross (see *34*), formerly Sparkford, with the medieval hospital and brothers' lodgings of the twelfth to fifteenth century (summer 09.30-12.30, 14.00-17.00, winter 10.30-12.30, 14.00-15.30). The walk through the watermeadows to St Cross inspired Keats to write his poem 'To Autumn'. Remains of the Itchen Navigation, especially St Catharine's lock, are of interest and can form part of a walk south of the city to St Catharine's Hill. There are fine nineteenth-century streets and churches, especially Christ Church and Christchurch Road, in the western area of the suburb.

East

Beyond the City Bridge is the eastern suburb. In Chesil Street (right) is The Soke, a seventeenth-century house (**29**; see *3*). Next to it is the medieval church of St Peter, Chesil, now a theatre. Almost opposite is the Old Chesil Rectory, an unusual medieval building (**30**).

Behind it are relics of the Great Western (Chesil) station yard and tunnels (**31**). In St John Street is the eponymous church (**32**), the best-preserved medieval parish church in the city. Above it is the Blue Boar (**33**; see *46*), a fourteenth-century hall house. St John's

Croft across the road is a splendid Georgian house (**34**). Proceed up the hill to St Giles Hill, site of the medieval fair and with unrivalled panoramic views of the city. Beyond St Giles Hill is Winnall (now a housing and industrial estate) where significant prehistoric, Roman and Saxon cemeteries have been found.

North

To the north lies the suburb of Hyde. The largest Roman cemeteries were here and remains of the abbey of Hyde (**35**) which removed there from the centre of town in *c.*1110. Fragments of abbey stonework are to be seen in adjacent buildings and in the church of St Bartholomew. An unmarked grave in the churchyard beside the east window may contain remains of King Alfred, scattered at the Reformation. The Hyde Abbey Resources centre is at 75 Hyde Street, and houses the Winchester City Museum Service and its extensive collections of photographs, local history room and the offices of the City Archaeologists.

WINCHESTER CHRONOLOGY

10,000-3700 BC: Palaeolithic and Mesolithic: Winchester area not a focus of population

3700-2000 BC: Neolithic: marked increase in activity both within the area later walled in and on the surrounding hills

2000-700 BC. Bronze Age: activity all round the city from *c.*2000 BC

700-300 BC: Early Iron Age: agricultural settlements in the area; hillfort at St Catharine's Hill

*c.*600-300 BC: settlement at Erdberi (Oram's Arbour)

*c.*300-100 BC: Middle Iron Age: settlement on downland in Itchen valley; Erdberi enclosed

*c.*100 BC–AD 43: Late Iron Age: St Catharine's hillfort abandoned (*c.*100 BC); dense population and industrial activity at Erdberi followed by decline; Winchester hoard of gold torcs etc. from this period

AD 43: Roman invasion of Britain by Claudius: Romans settle area of Venta beside Itchen (*c.*50)

After *c.*70: Venta Belgarum accorded *civitas* status

*c.*75: defences built on north, south (including South Gate) and west

*c.*150: first written references to Venta Belgarum

*c.*180-200: earthwork defences enclose *c.*58ha (144 acres), including east perimeter; earliest defences very dilapidated by this time

Before 200: Itchen diverted and bridged east of the city

300s: bastions added to defences

*c.*330-50: possible Christian chi-rho motif in archaeological record alongside paganism; thriving and populous town

*c.*350: textile *gynaecaeum* based at 'Venta'; town-house culture declining

By 380: drainage system failing, some streets going out of use

Late 300s: great town houses demolished/adapted

*c.*300-410: first Saxon cemeteries

*c.*400-50: little archaeological evidence; city all but abandoned by 450

After 500: pagan Saxon cemeteries outside city walls

Late 500s/early 600s: South Gate blocked

*c.*600 to after 700: Saxon cemeteries continue

635: arrival of Christian missionary Birinus in Wessex

642-73: King Cenwalh reigns; return of Christianity

648: traditional date for foundation of Old Minster

660: Bishop Wine, the first known bishop of Winchester, appointed

*c.*650-700: Christian female burial at Lower Brook Street

*c.*700 foundation of Saxon Southampton

757: first reference to Hampshire, the earliest shire

860: Viking attack on Winchester

861x3: death of Bishop Swithun

871-99: reign of King Alfred: Winchester mint evidence late in reign; buried at Winchester

896: Alfred's only recorded visit to Winchester

899-924: reign of Edward the Elder; buried at Winchester

901: foundation of New Minster

963: Bishop Aethelwold (died 984) elected to Winchester by King Edgar (959-75)

Before 980: establishment of Wolvesey, bishop's residence

980: rededication of Old Minster, converted to monasticism, by Aethelwold

1016-35: reign of Cnut: buried at Old Minster

1042: Harthacnut buried at Winchester

*c.*1057: population of city 5500-8000

1066: Battle of Hastings and Norman Conquest; Winchester opens its gates to the Conqueror

1069: rebellion against William I; Stigand removed as Bishop of Winchester and Archbishop of Canterbury (1070) and imprisoned at new Winchester castle (1072)

1079-80: Winchester cathedral begun by Bishop Walkelin (1070-98)

1093: dedication of the cathedral, otherwise St Swithun's priory church; Swithun's remains removed from Old Minster which was demolished

1100-29: William Giffard bishop; building at cathedral and Wolvesey

1107: cathedral tower collapses

*c.*1110: 1300 houses, second only to London: New Minster moves to northern suburb of Hyde

1129-71: Henry of Blois bishop: buildings at Wolvesey; St Cross (*c.*1135); Winchester Bible (*c.*1160)

1135-54: reign of Stephen: civil war and anarchy; city besieged and severely damaged (1141)

1148: survey of Winchester: 1100 houses; 57 parish churches

1154-89: reign of Henry II: royal 'Hawkheye' built north-west of city; castle works (1170s)

1189-99: reign of Richard I: coronations at Winchester in 1189 and 1194; charter

1199-1216: reign of John; reign ends with civil war and siege of castle; charter

*c.*1200: city seal shows crenellated gates; first reference to a mayor

1205-38: Peter des Roches bishop

1207: Henry III (1216-72) born at Winchester

1222-36: castle great hall built: Peter des Roches a prime mover

1227: Henry III of age: charter promises perpetual mint at Winchester

1231: Bishop des Roches returns to England; established The Soke – separate jurisdiction

1248-50: final closure of mint

1250-60: Aymer de Lusignan (de Valence) bishop: created rich Purbeck screen to enclose Swithun's shrine, also Purbeck heart-burial memorial to Aymer

1258: barons besiege bishop in Wolvesey

1261: Winchester parliament in great hall

1264: citizens attack priory burning King's and Prior's gates; Henry III acts to protect Jews in city

1265: capture of city by Simon de Montfort the younger

1285: Statute of Winchester

1290: expulsion of Jews from England by Edward I

*c.*1290: earliest date for timber of Round Table, and earliest dated timber framed house in Winchester at 42 Chesil Street

*c.*1300 population in range 8000-11,625

1302: royal visit and fire at castle

1326-53: Winchester a wool staple town

1338-9: wall works inspired by recent French coastal raids

1344: foundation of the Order of the Round Table; radio-carbon date for creation of Round Table

1345-66: William Edington bishop; demolished westworks of Norman cathedral by 1350

1348-50: Black Death kills 48 per cent of clergy in diocese: very severe effects in the city; 'a turning point' for Winchester

1366-1404: William of Wykeham bishop

1369: royal order for repair of walls

1377-99: Richard II king; visits Winchester 1393, feasts with Wykeham

1377-81: poll tax levied

1377: French land on south coast; Durn Gate walled up

1381: Great Revolt: violence in Winchester

1382: Wykeham receives royal licence to obtain lands for Winchester College

1387-1401: Chamber Court (1387-94) and Outer Court (1397-1401) at Winchester College built

1393: parliament summoned to Winchester

1399-1413: Henry IV king; visits Winchester in 1402 to marry Joan of Navarre

1417: tarrage roll gives population figure of 7-8000

1447: death of Bishop Beaufort who had rebuilt the Hospital of St Cross for his retainers' retirement

1440-52: petition twice sent to king complaining of 11 almost depopulated streets, 997 empty houses, 17 churches without incumbents etc.; withdrawal of cloth industry

1447-86: William Waynflete bishop

c.1475-90: Waynflete's great screen in cathedral

1476: relics of Swithun paraded through the city *en route* to new shrine

1486: Tudor Henry VII has his first son Arthur christened at Winchester

1493-1501: Thomas Langton bishop: died of plague; chantry chapel, completed by successor Fox (1501-28) contains perhaps the earliest 'Renaissance work' in England

1522: Emperor Charles V visits Winchester with Henry VIII; probable date of painting of Round Table

1524: population 2000-4300

1531-51, 1553-5: Stephen Gardiner bishop

1530s: early attempt at Itchen Navigation fails

1538-40: Dissolution of monasteries: destruction of Waynflete's screen, Swithun's shrine and monastic buildings at cathedral priory, Hyde and St Mary's Abbey, friaries etc.

1551: citizens acquire East Gate and income from its tolls from successors of St Mary's Abbey

1554: Queen Mary married to Philip of Spain in the cathedral

1566: tailors and hosiers seek protection against rural craftsmen

1579: county workhouse established at the castle with encouragement from Sir Francis Walsingham (made High Steward of city, 1582)

1583: first outbreak of plague for almost 20 years

1588: Charter of Incorporation

1591 (and 1604): earliest references to horse-racing at Winchester

1594-5: corporation bought wheat and rye for the poor to eat; wool and flax for them to work for wages

1597: burials in St Maurice and in northern suburb reach epidemic proportions

1603: religious census found twice as many recusants (Catholics) as nonconformists in Winchester: 1851 communicants

1603-6: plague in the city and suburbs

1615: Symonds's almshouse opens

1620s: Winchester fails to get Itchen Navigation accepted

1625: worst plague in the city since Black Death

1632-47: Walter Curle bishop: oversaw creation of cathedral tower vault, decorated *c.*1635; Inigo Jones screen and Laudian altar canopy

1642-6: Civil War: city attacked and pillaged by both sides; royalists in castle surrender to Waller; parliamentarians under Waller defeat Hopton at Cheriton; refugees flee to castle; Cromwell arrives, takes suburbs easily and bombards castle; Ogle surrenders (1645). Population falls to under 5000

1649: Charles I executed; royalist city government replaced

1651: castle demolished

1660: Restoration greeted with joy in city; Catholic burials at St James cemetery begin

1660-2: Brian Duppa bishop; begins rebuilding Wolvesey

1662-84: Bishop Morley repairs Wolvesey and donates his library to the cathedral; new clergy houses built in The Close, replacing losses during Interregnum

1662: reforming commissioners eject 1649 government

1664: Itchen Navigation included in a bill, but limited after Southampton's intervention (to the port's benefit), to coal and 'the Norway trade'

1665: hearth tax: population estimate 5900

1666: serious plague: pit-cairns still visible south of St Catharine's Hill

1668: hearth tax farmers cite Winchester as a city where receipts had fallen due to the plague

1674: nine canons lived in houses with ten or more hearths: Morley College for clergy widows built

1676: Compton 'census', estimated population 3700

1680s: Charles II's patronage makes city a centre for upper-class society

1682: Charles II and court attend races at Winchester: palace plans hatched

1685: Charles II dies: palace building halts

1686: stabling survey: Winchester has stabling for 1000+ horses, far outstrips other Hampshire towns

1704: 90 shops assessed within the walls for land tax: 20 substantial houses in the city

1710: Itchen Navigation opened

1714: new guildhall sponsored by Queen Anne

1725: visitation suggests rising population, especially in suburbs: 4000

1750: Godson: first measured map of city

1771: Winchester Pavement Commission established to oversee paving, lighting etc. of streets

1788: population at visitation 3500-4000

1801: census gives population of 6069

1838: Corn Exchange in Jewry Street opens

1839: railway from Southampton opens

1840: link to Basingstoke opens through route to London. Diocesan Training College founded

1841: census gives population of 9889

1845: British Archaeological Association and Institute meet (separately) in Winchester

1845-52: Carter reworks Great Hall and remodels grand jury chamber, Castle Yard

1851: census gives population of 12,042; Bishop's Cheyney Court ceased to function

1868-72: large-scale Ordnance Survey Map of the city

1873: new guildhall completed on The Broadway

1875: sewage pumping station established at Garnier Road

1885: Didcot, Newbury and Southampton Junction Railway (G.W.R.) opens at Winchester

1888: creation of Hampshire County Council

1891: census gives population of 19,670

1894: fire destroys Charles II's palace

1899: Prince of Wales lays foundation stone of new barracks at palace site

1901: census gives population of 20,143

1903: opening of Winchester Museum in The Square

1914-18: First World War: 459 military and naval personnel gave their lives in a tradition of 'service and sacrifice handed down from King Alfred'

1920s: new housing at Stanmore wins national acclaim

1928: Diocesan Training College becomes King Alfred's College

1930s: depression, little building in the city

1939-45: Second World War: Dunkirk evacuees housed at the barracks; Winchester bypass a useful link especially at D-Day (1944); destruction and post-war depression provide opportunities for archaeology

1951: census gives populaton of 25,721

1959: Queen Elizabeth Court County Council buildings opened

1962-71: Winchester Excavations Committee organises archaeology in the city

1971: census gives population of 31,107

1982: 600th anniversary of the foundation of Winchester College

Late 1980s: Winchester dubbed 'the wealthiest city in Britain'

1991: census gives population of 29,758

1990s: 'rescue' and 'research' archaeology in the city give way to planning-led work under PPG 16; Twyford Down revolt characterises local concerns and growing awareness of historic environment

2001: census gives population of 34,736

2005: University of Winchester established by order of the Privy Council

BIBLIOGRAPHY

Publications relating to Winchester including books, museum newsletters and journal articles are listed in *Winchester: a bibliography* by Susan C. Browne (Winchester Project, King Alfred's College, 1993 updated by Mark Allen 1996). This is available at the Hampshire Record Office. It is in two parts, organised by subject and by author. The first edition of my text in common with the practice of the Batsford/English Heritage series did not contain textnotes or footnotes, but these are included here. The bibliography below is also in two parts. First, a selection of works used in the 1997 edition, but which are only exceptionally cited in this revised text. Second, a selection of works used for this edition, many post-1997, which are cited and listed in the second part of this Bibliography.

SELECT WORKS IN 1997 EDITION

Archaeological Institute. *Proceedings of the Annual Meeting of the Archaeological Institute Of Great Britain and Ireland Held at Winchester, September MDCCCXLV*. (London 1846) contains R. Willis 'The Architectural History of Winchester Cathedral'; C.R. Cockerell 'The Architectural Works of William of Wykeham'; C. Winton on painted glass; J.H. Parker on architecture; E. Hawkins on mints and moneyers; E. Smirke on the Round Table and Castle Hall, and E.A. Freeman on the architecture of St Cross

Atkinson, T., *Elizabethan Winchester* (London 1963)

Anglo-Saxon Chronicle ed. J. Stevenson in *The Church Historians of England* Volume II.i (London 1853)

Ball, C., *An Historical Account of Winchester With Descriptive Walks* (Winchester 1818)

Barlow, F., Biddle, M., von Feilitzen, O. and Keene, D. J., *Winchester in the Early Middle Ages: an edition and discussion of the Winton Domesday,* Winchester Studies 1 (Oxford 1976)

Biddle, M., (ed.) *Object and Economy in Medieval Winchester,* Winchester Studies 7.ii (2 vols Oxford 1990)

Biddle, M., The Study of Winchester: archaeology and history in a British Town, 1961-1983', *Proceedings of the British Academy* 69 (1983), pp.93-135

Biddle, M., *Wolvesey: the old bishop's palace, Winchester* (London 1986)

Biddle, M., 1968 'Archaeology and history of British Towns' *Antiquity* 42, 109-16

Boorman, W., 1990, 'Health and sanitation in Victorian Winchester: or the triumph of the Muckabites' *Proceedings of the Hampshire Field Club and Archaeological Society*, 16-180

Carpenter Turner, B., *Winchester* (Chichester, reprinted 1990, revised 1992)

Clarke, G., *Pre-Roman and Roman Winchester, Part II: The Roman Cemetery at Lankhills* Winchester Studies 3.ii (Oxford 1979)

Collis, J., *Winchester Excavations 1949-1960, volume ii* (Winchester 1978)

Crook, J., *Winchester Cathedral: Nine Hundred Years* (Chichester 1993)

Crook, J., (ed.) *The Wainscot Book* (Hampshire Record Series, 6, Winchester 1984)

Cunliffe, B., *Winchester Excavations 1949-1960, volume i* (Winchester 1964)

Davey, C.R. (ed.) *The Hampshire Lay Subsidy Rolls, 1586* (Hampshire Record Series 4, 1981)

Defoe, D., *A Tour Through the Whole Island of Great Britain* (London 1731/1964)

Donovan, C., *The Winchester Bible* (London and Winchester 1993)

Fiennes, C., *The Illustrated Journeys of Celia Fiennes, 1685-c.1712*, ed. Morris, C., (London 1982)

Freeman, R. *The Art and Architecture of Owen Browne Carter (1806-1859)* Hampshire Papers 1 (Winchester 1991)

Fryde, E.B., Greenaway, D.E., Porter, S. and Roy, I., (eds) *Handbook of British Chronology* (3rd edition, London, 1986)

Hockey, S.F. (ed.) *The Register of William Edington* (Hampshire Record Series 7 and 8, 1986, 1987)

Hughes, E. and White, P., (eds) *The Hampshire Hearth Tax Assessment 1665* (Hampshire Record Series, 1981)

Hyde, H., *Some Account of the Tombs and Monuments in the Cathedral Church of Winchester* (London 1683, reprinted with a catalogue 1715)

James, T.B., *Winchester: a pictorial history* (Chichester 1993)

James, T.B., 'The population size of Winchester over 2,000 years: a survey' *Hampshire Field Club and Archaeological Society section newsletters* (New Series, 9 1988), 1-3

Keene, D.J., *A Survey of Medieval Winchester* Winchester Studies 2 (2 vols Oxford 1985)

Kjlbye-Biddle, B., 'Dispersal or concentration – the disposal of the Winchester dead over 2000 years' in Bassett, S., *Death in Towns 100-1600* (Leicester 1993)

Lewis, E., Roberts, E. and Roberts, K., *Medieval Hall Houses of the Winchester Area* (Winchester 1988)

Oldfield, J., *Printers, Booksellers and Libraries in Hampshire, 1750-1800* Hampshire Papers 3 (Winchester 1993)

Pevsner, N. and Lloyd, D., *Hampshire*, Buildings of England Series (London 1967)

Qualmann, K.E., 'Roman Winchester' in Greep, S., (ed.) *Roman Towns: the Wheeler inheritance*, CBA Research Report 93 (1993)

Ranger, P., *The Georgian Playhouses of Hampshire 1730-1830* Hampshire Papers 10 (Winchester 1995)

Rosen, A., 'Winchester in Transition 1580-1700' in Clark P., (ed.) *Country Towns in Pre-Industrial England* (Leicester 1981) 144-195

Rosen A., Economic and social aspects of the history of Winchester 1520-1670 (DPhil thesis, University of Oxford 1975)

Scobie, G. and Qualmann, K., *Nunnaminster: a Saxon and medieval community of nuns* (Winchester 1993)

Scobie, G.D., Zant, J.M. and Whinney, R., *The Brooks, Winchester: a preliminary report on the excavations 1987-88* Winchester Museums Service – Archaeology Report 1 (Winchester 1991)

Spence, M., *Hampshire and Australia, 1783-1791: crime and transportation* Hampshire Papers 2 (Winchester 1992)

Stedman, J., Some aspects of the economic history of Winchester, 1770-1810 (unpublished MA dissertation, Leicester 1979)

Stevenson, M., *Weights and Measures of the City of Winchester* (Winchester ed.)

Taylor, J., 'Plague in the towns of Hampshire: the plague of 1665-6' *Southern History* 4, (1984), 105-15

Temple Patterson, A., *A History of Southampton. Volume III: Setbacks and Recoveries, 1868-1914* (Southampton Records Series 18, 1975)

Vickers, J.A., (ed.), *The Religious Census of 1851* (Hampshire Record Series 12, 1993)

Victoria County History

von Feilitzen in Barlow *et al.*, 1991, 185-9

ADDITIONAL WORKS IN THIS EDITION

Allen, M.A., 'A Railway Revolution? A census-based analysis of the economic, social and topographical effects of the coming of the railway upon the city of Winchester *c.* 1830 to *c.* 1890' (Unpublished PhD thesis, King Alfred College of Higher Education, Winchester, for the University of Southampton, 1999)

Arthur, P. A., 'The impact of the Black Death on seventeen units of account of the bishopric of Winchester' (Unpublished PhD thesis, University College, Winchester, for the University of Southampton, 2005)

Atkins, C.A, 'Study of Military Monuments and Service in First World War Winchester' (Unpublished BA dissertation, King Alfred's College, Winchester, 1999 with a database of the Roll of Honour for The Winchester Project)

Biddell, B., *The Jolly Farmer? William Cobbett in Hampshire 1804-1820*, Hampshire Papers 15 (Winchester 1999)

Biddle, M., *King Arthur's Round Table* (Woodbridge 2000)

Biddle, M. and Clayre, B., *Winchester Castle and Great Hall* (Hampshire County Council 1983 new edition 2000)

Birkbeck, V. and Moore, C., 'Preservation and Investigation of Roman and Medieval Remains at Hyde Street, Winchester' *Hampshire Studies* 59 2004 77-111

Cooper, J.M., 'Aspects of the Development of Winchester's High Street 1550-2000' (2 volumes. Unpublished PhD thesis, King Alfred's College of Higher Education, Winchester, for the University of Southampton, 2001)

Crossley, P.A., 'Winchester Corporation Leases in the early Nineteenth Century: a Review of Financial Aspects as a Source of City Building History' (Unpublished PhD thesis, King Alfred's College of Higher Education, Winchester, for the University of Southampton, 2003)

Cunliffe, B., *The Celts* (Oxford 2003)

Dunhill, R., *Handel and the Harris Circle* Hampshire Papers 8 (Winchester 1995)

Gapper, C., Parker, K. and Roberts, E., 'Elizabethan and Jacobean Decorative Features at Hyde, Winchester' *Hampshire Studies,* 57 2002, 59-80

Gerrard, C., *Medieval Archaeology: understanding traditions and contemporary approaches* (London 2003)

Hare, J., 'Winchester College and the Angel Inn Andover: a fifteenth-century landlord and its investments' *Hampshire Studies,* 59 2005, 187-97

Harwood, W., 'The Household of Winchester College in the Later Middle Ages 1400-1560' *Hampshire Studies,* 59 2005, 163-79

HCC, *A Goodly Heritage: Hampshire Record Office 1947-1997* (Winchester 1997)

Henderson, I. and Crook, J. *The Winchester Diver* (Crawley 1984)

Hinde, A. and Turnbull, F. 'The populations of two Hampshire workhouses, 1851-1861' *Local Population Studies* 61 1998, 38-53

James, T. B., 'The Black Death: a turning point for Winchester?' *Hatcher Review,* 46 1998 32-42

James, T. B. and Gerrard, C. M., *The King's Landscape: rediscovering Clarendon Park, Wiltshire* (Macclesfield 2007)

James, T. B. and Roberts, E. V., 'Winchester and Late-Medieval Urban Development: from palace to pentice' *Medieval Archaeology* 44 2000, 181-200

Lapidge, M., *The Cult of St Swithun* (Oxford 2003)

Lewis, E. and and Turle, R., 'Early Domestic Wall Paintings in Hampshire' *Hampshire Studies,* 60 2006, 202-219

Kent, D., *Popular Radicalism and the Swing Riots in Central Hampshire* Hampshire Papers 11 (Winchester 1997)

May, M., 'Winchester Houses and People *c.* 1650-*c.* 1710: a study based on probate evidence' (Unpublished PhD thesis, King Alfred's College of Higher Education, Winchester, for the University of Southampton, 1998)

Moxley, C., *An Introduction to the History of St Paul's Hospital, Winchester* (Winchester 1987)

Patten, B., *Catholicism and the Gothic Revival* Hampshire Papers 21 (Winchester 2001)

Roberts E., *Hampshire Houses 1250-1700: their dating and development* (Winchester 2003)

Sherlock, R. 'Chandeliers in Hampshire and Isle of Wight Churches: a Gazetteer' *Hampshire Studies,* 60 2006

Stedman, M., 'Two Germanic migration period metalwork pieces from St Cross Winchester, Hampshire' *Hampshire Studies* 59 2004

Thomson, A., 'Estate Management in the Winchester Diocese before and after the Interregnum: a missed opportunity' *Hampshire Studies,* 60 2006, 184-201

Watts, D.G. 'The Black Death in Dorset and Hampshire' *Hatcher Review,* 46 1998, 21-28

Winchester Museums Service, *Ice to Iron: Prehistoric Peoples in Hampshire* (Winchester 2003)

Winchester Museums Service, *Venta Belgarum: The Roman Town of Winchester* (Winchester 1997)

Winchester Museums Service, *Winchester: Into the Modern Age* (Winchester 2001a)

Winchester Museums Service, *Wintanceaster: Saxon and Medieval Winchester* (Winchester 2001b)

Yorke, B., *The King Alfred Millenary in Winchester, 1901* Hampshire Papers 17 (Winchester 1999)

www.channel4.com/history/microsites/T/timeteam/archive/2001win.html
www.cityofwinchester.co.uk/history
www.hants.gov.uk/factsandfigures/winchester for 2001 and 2006 census
www.winchestermuseums.org, 2006 Winchester Museums Service
www.winchester.gov.uk for Hyde Community Archaeology Project
www.workhouses.org.uk for Winchester workhouse maps etc.

INDEX